# Basics of ...

# STARTING
# A FLORIDA
# BUSINESS

# Basics of ...

# STARTING A FLORIDA BUSINESS

## An Explanation For Everyday People

### Albert L. Kelley, Esq.

Basics of ...
A Basic Knowledge Imprint of
ABSOLUTELY AMAZING eBOOKS

# Basics of ...

is an imprint of
ABSOLUTELY AMAZING eBOOKS

Published by Whiz Bang LLC, 926 Truman Avenue, Key West, Florida 33040, USA

*Basics of ... Starting a Florida Business* copyright © 2018 by Albert L. Kelley, Esq. Electronic compilation/ print edition copyright © 2018 by Whiz Bang LLC.

For information contact:
Publisher@AbsolutelyAmazingEbooks.com

ISBN-13: 978-1949504026 (Basics of ...)
ISBN-10: 1949504026

# Basics of ...

# STARTING A FLORIDA BUSINESS

# THANKS

This book was written with the help of my wonderful wife and first copy editor, Angie Kelley, who has been correcting my mistakes for over two decades.

# Table of Contents

# INTRODUCTION

The law should not be a mystery. It is what has guided our Country since it's founding. Yet so many lawyers want to make you think that it is something only professionals can understand. The law is there for everyone and should not be complicated. That being said, there are nuances that may create some questions. The purpose of this book is to give some guidance on the requirements to start your own business. The book will start with the initial planning and follow through to opening day. If you have an interest in starting a new business, whether that means starting from scratch or taking over an existing business, by the end of this series, you should have all the tools you need.

Let me begin by giving you my background. My name is Al Kelley and I am a lawyer, magistrate, mediator, author, businessman, and book publisher. I spent several years as a college professor for St. Leo University, teaching among other things, business law. I graduated with honors from Florida State University in 1989 and have been practicing law ever since. I have handled cases focusing on business law, real estate, corporations, entertainment law, contracts, landlord-tenant law, foreclosures, copyrights, and trademarks. My clients have included individuals and companies. I have litigated cases in the County, Circuit and Appellate Courts of Florida for both Plaintiff and

Defendants. I have been a state certified mediator for over ten years and a Judicial Magistrate for three. I was also the Chairman of the Monroe County Career Service Council- a quasi-judicial agency. I am a member of the Florida Bar, and have been a member of the Trial Bar of the United States District Court for the Southern and Middle Districts of Florida. I also am the owner or co-owner of numerous companies. I have written a weekly newspaper column on business law for three different publications, as well as authoring three prior legal books, and teaching at numerous seminars.

Now for the mandatory disclaimer. The information being provided in this book is not designed to be specific legal advice. It is offered for information purposes only. It is not oriented towards any specific issue and through it, I am not representing any person or entity. The principles presented are based on Florida law although it may apply just as well in other states (I am not licensed to practice in any other state and do not profess to be an expert on the laws of other states). While I will discuss the law to some extent, this book cannot and does not replace legal advice and legal counsel. If you have a specific legal issue that you need advice on, consult with an attorney of your choice.

I hope you find this book informative and entertaining, but mostly, I hope you find it useful.

# STARTING A BUSINESS FROM SCRATCH

**S**tarting a business from scratch is an entrepreneur's dream. However, it requires an amazing amount of planning, work, and faith.   Of course, this column cannot discuss how to start every type of business, but there are certain actions which are common to almost any type of business.

Let's start with initial planning. While it is helpful to know what type of business you want to start, it is not always required.   Many business people start as investors, buying an available business, even if they have no experience in that field.   This is often seen in the restaurant industry.   Although the restaurant industry is extremely complicated and has a high failure rate, many people believe they have the ability to succeed (According to a 2016 study, restaurants have the third highest failure rate among all sectors, and the main reason for failure is incompetence).   For those willing to do the work and study the industry, advance knowledge of the industry is not always required. You can also often put clauses in the purchase agreement requiring the seller to assist with the transition and provide basic training.

If however you are planning on starting the business

from scratch, failure to know the industry in advance is a recipe for failure. So this is where you make your first decisions: Do you want to start a business from scratch or buy an existing business? And do you know anything about the type of business you want to open?

There are countless issues to consider when making these initial decisions.

1. Do you want to open a particular type of business? If not, you can simply look for any business that is for sale. But if you want to open a particular type of business, your options may be too limited to do anything but open your own.

2. Does the business you want open already exist? If not, you have no choice but to open your own business.

3. If so, is the business for sale? If there are no businesses in your industry listed for sale, you may be required to start your own.

4. How much are you willing to invest? If you want to buy an existing business, how much will it cost? There is an old adage that everything is for sale at the right price, but the right price might be too high. Plus, there are operational costs that need to be added to the initial purchase price. If you are interested in starting your own business, there are start-up costs that must be considered. You must ensure that you have enough capital to cover the business through opening and preferably for the first several months of operations until the business can cover its own costs. Aside from the issue of not being able to cover the cost of the business, there are legal reasons for this question. If a business is undercapitalized, the Courts can allow creditors or others with lawsuits against the

business to pierce the corporate veil and sue the owners directly. More on that later.

5. Intangibles. With every start-up business there are unique issues that you may not have thought of. Keep flexible and creative to get over those hurdles as they arise.

As you can see, the initial planning is not simple. Yet, it need to be done, and done in detail. Otherwise, you may be throwing your investment money away.

Every scratch business starts with planning. Planning is not a short term activity. It is a continuing activity, that begins well before the business is started. If it is not done, the business will fail. I know of no successful business that didn't start without a basic plan.

I am assuming you have an idea what type of business you want to create. First you must know whether the principles of the business are required to have certain status, degree or training. As an example, while it may sound obvious, only lawyers may own a law firm. If it sounds obvious, why is it an issue? Perhaps a lawyer wants to make his non-lawyer wife a shareholder in his law firm. It would not be allowed. Or what if a lawyer and accountant want to start a law firm to help form new companies. This would also not be allowed as the accountant (even a CPA), although a professional and relevant to business formation, is not a lawyer. Nearly all professional companies can only be owned by people holding the appropriate degrees. But this also has importance for other businesses. Construction companies have to have a contractor; real estate companies must have a broker. For many businesses, no training is required. There are no required degrees or education to open up a retail store, or a restaurant, or a dog walking business. If the business requires a status that you do not have, change the type of business you want to create.

The next decision is the type of business entity you want to use.

There are numerous types of business entities to consider, but the five main entity types are sole proprietorships, partnerships, C-corporations, S-corporations, and Limited Liability companies. Each type has its advantages and disadvantages. We will discuss these options later.

# BUYING AN EXISTING BUSINESS

**B**uying an existing business comes with a tremendous number of decisions and agreements. While most people think the price is the most important issue to consider, it is just one of many.

Often a buyer will start with visiting a realtor. This is a common practice, but requires research. Just as many lawyers specialize in areas of law, realtors often specialize in various types of transactions. Some focus on residential properties; some focus on commercial properties; and others focus on businesses. Make sure the realtor you are working with has experience in business transactions. Buying a business is not the same as buying real estate, and realtors unfamiliar with the differences will often use improper documentation, such as trying to manipulate a residential sales contract to cover the business sale.

Another issue that you find with inexperienced realtors is valuation. Unlike real estate, it is not as easy to determine an appropriate price to pay for a business. While real estate values can be calculated by comparing the sales of similar properties, each business is unique and relies on a combination of factors such as type of business, size of commercial space, experience of owner, and location of store. With purchasing an existing business, you are also buying that business' goodwill- the business' reputation.

The goodwill may be different than expected, resulting in a higher or lower value. There may be actions in the prior business that will not become apparent until later that will have an effect on the reputation. Also, if a person is willing to sell an existing business, you should wonder why they are willing to sell. Is the business not as successful as they imply? Are there unstated problems? Employee issues? Landlord issues? If starting your own business, how long will it take to build up goodwill? How will you attract new customers? How easy will it be to get financing?

Comparing two businesses in different parts of town is like comparing apples to oranges. Some realtors will try to estimate what a reasonable price should be for the business. Be careful when accepting this value. Business valuation is a specialty practice that requires detailed knowledge of the assets of the business, the accounting of the business, and the market. While some website will say there are only three or four ways to value a business, in actuality there are numerous methods. The primary valuation methods are the Asset Method, where you calculate the value of all the hard assets of the company, the Market Approach, where you look at what other businesses in the area have sold for, and the Multiple of Gross Income where the gross income of the business is increased by a fixed multiplier. There are also the Discounted Cash Flow method, the Return On Investment method, the Price-to-Earning method, the Earnings Before Taxes method, and the Multiple of Gross Income. However, at the end of the day, most businesses are sold simply based on what one person wants to receive and another person is willing to pay.

The next question to ask is whether to buy an existing

corporation (or LLC), or whether to just buy the assets. As a general rule, Sellers want to sell their stock in the corporation; Buyers want to buy the assets. Why? If you buy the stock or membership of a company or LLC, you are getting the assets, but you are also getting the liabilities. If the Seller hasn't paid their sales tax, you now owe it; if there was a slip and fall in the last two years, the Buyer may be buying a lawsuit. By buying only the assets, the Buyer gets all the benefits without the liabilities. The Seller continues to be liable for his debts and obligations. So why is this an issue? Why would anyone buy the stock or membership of the company? Sometimes the company itself brings benefits you don't get with just a purchase of the assets. For example the company may hold certain licenses that are not transferrable. Or the company may have a long history that the new owner wants to continue. This issue can also arise when the Seller only owns a majority stake in the company. Here the Seller can sell his majority interest, giving the Buyer control, even if minority shareholders don't agree to sell.

If buying the stock in a corporation, inspect carefully all the financial records of the company. There are a few reasons that the financials are crucial. First it helps determine the value of the business. Second, it can show the success or failure of the business. A store may do a lot of business, but still lose money. The financial records can show the health of the business. Third, it can give indications of where the business might be improved. After looking through the financials you may discover that the owner is paying too much for supplies. A reduction in spending may translate to a higher income and a better investment. Finally, is a risk analysis. If you buy the stock in a company, you become responsible for all the liabilities of that company. If the taxes have not been paid, the Buyer becomes liable for them; if inventory has not been paid, it may be repossessed, leaving the buyer without merchandise to sell. The financial records can clue you in to what pitfalls await you after closing. However, do not take the financials as a guarantee of income. Every business owner does thing differently. How the Buyer runs the business may be different than the seller. And even what seems a minor change can have massive impacts. The financial records merely show how a specific business was run by a specific person for a specific time.

Once you have decided if you are buying assets or stock, it is time to look at other issues related to the sale. Regardless of an asset sale or stock sale, the location of the business is the next major consideration. This starts with practical issues: is the business located in an area that is conducive to the business. A fishing business in a landlocked area may not work. Or a fine dining establishment in the industrial sector of a city may not succeed. For some businesses, location is irrelevant. If you are operating a home-based business, an internet-based business or a Post Office Box based business, location is less important. Another consideration is availability. If the business office space is owned by the seller and is part of the business purchase, this is less of an issue (Although your business plans may be to relocate the business). But, if the business is leased, the lease needs to be examined to determine if it is transferrable. Logic would tell you that if you but the stock of a company, you would automatically get to take over any leases in the company name. This is not necessarily the case. Most commercial leases have a clause against assignments without the landlord's consent. In addition, the leases usually also have a clause that states a transfer of stock is deemed an unauthorized assignment. In other words, if you buy stock in a company without the landlord's consent, it may be deemed a breach of the lease and subject you to eviction.

If you are purchasing the assets of a company, the lease is usually included in the assets. If the lease does not address the issue of assignment, the tenant may freely assign the lease to a new tenant. The law favors the free alienation of property. However, again, most of the time the lease requires the landlord's consent. The Landlord's obligation to consent to a lease assignment is governed by the lease. Almost always the lease will have some language regarding assignment. Rarely it will state that the lease is freely assignable. Most of the time, the Landlord's consent is necessary. However, the landlord's right to object may be limited. If the lease states that the Landlord may reject an assignment for any or no reason, his authority is absolute. But often the lease will say that the Landlord's consent will not be unreasonably withheld. What does that mean? The landlord can only look at certain issues regarding consent. In general, when considering the assignment, the landlord must apply standards of good faith and commercial reasonableness. To do this, the Landlord may consider the following factors: (a) financial responsibility of the proposed subtenant (b) the "identity" or "business character" of the subtenant, i.e., suitability for the particular building, (c) the need for alteration of the premises, (d) the legality of the proposed use, and (e) the nature of the occupancy, i.e., office, factory, clinic, etc. If the landlord rejects the lease assignment based on personal taste, convenience, or any other factor other than commercial reasonableness or if the landlord states they will only accept the assignment if the new tenant pays a higher rent, the landlord will have been deemed to be in breach of the lease and may be responsible for any damages the tenant incurs due to the rejection (By the way, if the lease says the landlord's consent is required but does not specify more than that, it will be deemed that the assignment will not be unreasonably withheld).

When the lease requires the Landlord's consent, it is recommended that the parties meet with the Landlord early in the negotiation process to ensure that the consent is obtained early before the parties invest substantial time and money.

# FRANCHISING

**A** hybrid of starting a business from scratch and buying an existing business is the franchise. Here you are in essence starting the business, but you are buying, or to be more truthful, licensing a name, trademark and know-how. There are 75 categories of franchises, including quick service restaurants (McDonalds), retail food (Outback), lodging (Doubletree), real estate (Century 21), retail products (Kilwans Chocolates), retail services (JiffyLube), business services (The UPS Store), and personal services (Sylvan Learning). There are roughly 3000 franchisors and around 750,000 franchisees in the country.

In a franchise situation, the business owner, called the franchisee, pays an upfront fee to the entity offering the franchise, called the franchisor. This upfront fee, called the franchise fee gives the franchisee the right to use the franchisor's business name, logo, business secrets, and know-how. It usually does not include the building, the equipment or inventory, although some franchisors will assist with finding a location, can lease equipment, and can provide inventory at a discount.

To start a franchise, each franchisor must create a document called a Uniform Franchise Offering Circular (UFOC). This is a detailed document that includes the identity of the franchisor along with its predecessors and affiliates, the names of the primary officers and directors of the franchisor, the history of the franchise, including all litigation and bankruptcies, a breakdown of all fees, including the initial franchise fee and any continuing fees, an estimate of the total initial investment, restrictions on merchandise/inventory-including what the franchisee may sell and where they may get their merchandise/inventory from, obligations of the franchisor and franchisee, a list of all of the franchisor's trademarks, patents and copyrights, renewal rights, and financial statements. This is a document that the franchisee must review carefully. Information in the UFOC can give the franchisee an idea if the franchise is a positive move.

Every franchise is different. Most franchise agreements provide an area of exclusivity where the franchisor will not allow any other franchises. For example, a franchisor may state that the franchisee has the exclusive right to operate that brand of store within a city. Or it may only limit the area to a square mile.

According to the International Franchise Association, the start-up cost of a franchise runs anywhere between $20,000 to over $1,000,000 (One report states that the start-up cost to open a McDonalds runs anywhere from $685,000-$1,504,000). 70% of all franchises have an initial franchise fee below $40,000 with the majority between $10,000 and $30,000. Many franchisors offer financing for these expenses. In addition to the start-up costs, most franchisors require the franchisees to pay a continuing monthly royalty. This could be a flat fee, but is usually a percentage of sales. Some franchisors require the franchisees to also pay a monthly advertising fee to allow the franchisor to create national or regional ads.

While there is often a high start-up cost, for a well-known franchise, the business is likely to turn a profit more quickly as customers will tend to go to a known business name before an unknown one. A franchise provides a known level of quality. No matter where you go, you know that McDonald's is going to offer a Big Mac that will be the same as the one from your home town. This gives the franchisee an immediate clientele.

While owning a franchise lets the franchisor own their own business, they still have to answer to the franchisor. This means they may have to follow instructions on how the store must look, what merchandise to sell, even how to display their merchandise. In addition, the franchisee cannot simply sell the business whenever they want. Franchisors have the right to approve or reject potential buyers, require the potential buyers to meet certain preconditions before a sale is allowed, or prevent the sale of the franchise outright. The reason for this is clear: franchisors are required to protect their trademarks, their operations and their reputations. If they fail to protect their trademarks, they run the risk of losing them; if they fail to protect the franchise reputation they risk lawsuits by their franchisees. This is why franchisors place restrictions on the stores such as product placement, marketing materials, store hours, etc.

At the same time, they must be careful not to exert too much control over the franchisee, lest they be deemed to be overreaching. If the franchisor puts too many controls on a franchisee, the courts can deem them to be partners, subjecting the franchisor to liability for the actions of the franchisee, even though the franchise agreement will clearly state the franchisee is an independent contractor. As an example, in a case from California, Patterson v Domino's, the appellate court held that Domino's Pizza was liable for its franchisee's actions in sexually harassing and wrongfully terminating an employee, when the franchise agreement put restrictions on the franchisee's hiring standards and where the franchisor could be involved in firing issues. The California Supreme Court reversed saying: "A franchisor enters this arena, and becomes potentially liable for actions of the franchisee's employees, only if it has retained or assumed a general right of control over factors such as hiring, direction, supervision, discipline, discharge, and relevant day-to-day aspects of the workplace behavior of the franchisee's employees. Any other guiding principle would disrupt the franchise relationship." Florida Courts have taken a similar approach. In the case of Domino's Pizza, LLC v. Wiederhold, decided just May 2018, the court stated "a franchisor may be held vicariously liable under an agency theory for the tortious acts of a franchisee, or a franchisee's employee, when the franchisor has direct control of, or the right to control, the day-to-day operations of the franchisee. See Mobil Oil Corp. v. Bransford, 648 So. 2d 119, 120 (Fla. 1995) (explaining that franchisor creates "agency relationship with a franchisee if, by contract or action or representation, the franchisor has directly or apparently participated in some substantial way in directing or managing acts of the franchisee"); Hickman v. Barclay's Int'l Realty, Inc., 5 So. 3d 804, 806 (Fla. 4th DCA 2009) (explaining it is right of control, not actual control or descriptive labels employed by parties, that determines agency relationship)". The Court stated it is up to a jury to determine whether the franchisor has liability for the actions of their franchisees.

# ASSET PURCHASE CONSIDERATIONS

**S**o now you have decided whether to purchase stock or assets, you have determined a fair price and you have confirmed that the lease is assignable. Time to look at other considerations.

Which assets are being purchased? Even if you are buying the stock, you will still be taking title to the assets. In some contracts they simply state "all assets"; in others they specify which assets are being transferred and which are not. Whichever way you choose to go, there should be a complete list of assets attached to the agreement. This is simply to avoid conflicts later. It is recommended that the list of assets be detailed. Rather than just listing "freezer" specify "Whirlpool chest style freezer, Model _____" or rather that stating "company truck" specify "2010 Ford F150, VIN_____". This guarantees that you receive the assets you inspected (There have been times when sellers swap out higher quality assets for less expensive ones when the list is not specific). The Buyer should also make a physical inspection of all assets rather than rely on the Seller to just provide a list. Even if the list is detailed, the assets themselves may not be in good condition, or may not match what the seller lists.

Another issue is to list things often not thought of.

Telephone numbers, Wi-Fi accounts, domain names, web pages, Facebook accounts, advertising materials. These assets make it easier for your customers to find you. Failure to include them can greatly harm the new business. If customers call the old telephone number and find it disconnected, they are not likely to come back. Or if the website is not transferred, people may look up the old website and find incorrect information.

What about intellectual property? This is usually an asset of the business, but may be held by the owner instead. Intellectual property includes trademarks, copyrights, patents and trade secrets. These can be extremely valuable and ultimately may eclipse the total value of the business (The value of the trademarks for the Coca Cola company exceed the value of every other asset in the company). Often owners will create a logo or trademark for the business but register it in their individual name. The same is true for copyrights, such as T-Shirt designs and advertising copy. If you buy the assets of the business, these copyrights would not be included unless the owner specifically includes them.

A related issue is whether the business even owns the trademark or copyrights. Under the existing copyright laws, ownership of a design or text belongs to the person who created it. This gets a little confusing. If a business owner has an idea for a logo and then hires a graphic artist to actually draw it, the graphic artist is deemed the owner of the copyright unless they assign those rights to the business. The same goes for advertising copy, menu design, etc. Unless the owner has an assignment of rights from the graphic artist, all they really own is a license to use the design. And the graphic artist is free to sell the same design to anyone they choose.

Trade secrets are just that: secrets. These include client lists, supplier lists, workbooks, and any business method that is not generally known outside the business. If the business has trade secrets, make sure they have taken steps to protect them, such as making employees sign confidentiality agreements.

Does the sale include fixtures? A fixture is a piece of equipment used for the business that is actually attached to the building. This can include shelving, cabinets, ceiling fans, etc. We have already discussed the lease. Now it is time to review it again. What does it say about fixtures? Most commercial leases state that fixtures belong to the landlord, and the general rule is that fixtures belong to the landlord when the tenant leaves the property. However, this is not always the case. Trade fixtures, that is, those items specifically installed for the business purpose, like hood systems for kitchens, bars, sinks, etc. remain the tenant's property, unless stated otherwise in the lease.

# NON-COMPETITION NON-SOLICITATION NON-DISCLOSURE AGREEMENTS

**W**hen drafting an Asset Sale Agreement or a Business Purchase Agreement, after you know exactly what assets are being bought, the price that will be paid and whether the lease is assignable, there are just a few other considerations which really need to be considered. The first is whether to include a Non-competition/ Non-solicitation/ Non-disclosure Agreement. This should be considered whenever a business is purchased. Many times, Buyers will only ask for a non-competition clause, but that is only one-third of the equation. You also need the Nonsolicitation and Nondisclosure as well. What are these?

Let's start with the Non-Competition Agreement. This is just what it sounds like. An agreement by the Seller that after the business is sold, the Seller will not open another business within a certain area for a certain period of time that operates in competition with the Buyer's business. Look at it this way. In any successful business, the owner of the business gets known by his customers and if allowed to open a competing business, many of those customers may switch to his new shop. This would damage the value of the business that was purchased.

These agreements are considered restraint of trade agreements and therefore are not favored by the court. They need to be drafted as carefully and as succinctly as possible, or the Court may refuse to honor them. Basically, they have to be narrowly drawn so as to only limit the Seller to the amount needed to protect the value of the purchase. To do this, the agreement must be reasonable in time, space and scope. In other words, the Agreement cannot prevent the Seller from opening any business, anywhere, forever. The scope of the Agreement must be limited to those businesses that compete with the business being sold; must limit the location to the businesses market area; and must not be excessive in time. There are different types of noncompetition agreements and they have different restrictions. A noncompetition agreement with an ex-employee is deemed unreasonable if it exceeds one year. A noncompetition with a franchisee or licensee will be deemed unreasonable after three years. But for the purchase of a business, the noncompete can last up to five years before being deemed unreasonable. If the agreement exceeds five years, it will likely be denied by the Court, allowing the Seller to immediately compete with the Buyer. Often the noncompete agreement will include language that states that if a Court finds any aspect too restrictive, the Court can impose a reasonable restriction. This can prevent the agreement from being set aside.

A noncompetition agreement is important, but as mentioned above, it is only one-third of the equation.

Related to the Non-competition agreement is a Non-solicitation agreement. This agreement states that not only will the Seller not compete with the Buyer, they also will not try to convince any of the customers of the business, or any of the employees of the business, to move to another company (even a company the Seller has no interest in). If the Seller has been successful (and sometimes even if they haven't), they have often built a level of respect and loyalty from their customers and employees. If the Seller tries to convince them to take their business to a competitor, it will undermine the business that the Buyer purchased. This is even more crucial with regards to key employees. Just as the business owner has a following, the same is true with some key employees or independent contractors. A hair dresser that has fixed customers can leave a salon if enticed by the prior owner to move to another salon. It is also a breach of the duty of good faith that arises in every transaction.

Finally, and often the most important is a non-disclosure agreement. In almost every business there are trade secrets; those little bits of know-how that distinguish one business from another. These include things such as your customer and supplier lists, recipes, business expansion plans, franchise plans, building layout designs, employee job descriptions, etc. These are valuable assets that make up a large part of the sale of a business or its assets. The last thing a Buyer wants is for the Seller to start telling everyone how the business was run after the sale is complete. The Buyer clearly does not want his competitors knowing all his business secrets the day after the sale occurs.

In every business purchase agreement, the inclusion of these items need to be carefully considered. If a Seller refuses to agree to the terms of a noncompetition/ nonsolicitation/ nondisclosure agreement, it sends a red flag up that the Seller has other plans in mind that could greatly reduce the value of the business.

# TYPES OF BUSINESS ENTITIES

**N**ow it is time for one of the big decisions: what type of entity will own the business? This may be dictated by circumstances, but usually you can plan this out. The simplest structure is the sole proprietorship. This is simply an individual doing business. Many small businesses operate as sole proprietorships. The entity does not need to register with the Department of State unless they intend to use a business name other than the owner's name. There are no special filings with the IRS. All income and expenses are listed directly on the owner's personal tax return. This has two benefits- first, you do not need to pay an accountant to prepare a corporate tax return and a personal tax return. Second, corporate tax returns are due on March 15, while personal tax returns are due on April 15. So, a sole proprietorship has an additional month to prepare their tax returns. Finally, as the sole proprietor, the business owner answers only to himself.

But as with the number of advantages, there are at least an equal number of disadvantages. As a sole proprietor, the capital of the company is limited to the personal savings of the owner, or what the owner can borrow. Also, the owner has full liability for anything that happens. If someone has a slip and fall in the shop, the owner is personally liable for their injuries. While that can be compensated with insurance, if the damages exceed the insurance limits, everything the business owner owns is subject to seizure (except homestead property). Finally, as a sole proprietor, the business owner may have to work longer hours without someone else to take over occasionally.

A similar structure is the general partnership. In a general partnership, two or more people work together to operate the business. It is not incorporated, so no special formalities are required (although it is heavily recommended that a partnership agreement be drafted). Like with a sole proprietorship, a general partnership does not need to be registered with the Department of State, although the business name will still need to be registered. And similar to the sole proprietorship, all partners have personal liability for anything the business does, or anything your partner does in furtherance of the business. The one advantage a partnership has over the sole proprietorship is the additional capital. Instead of relying on the savings of one person to start the business, a partnership allows multiple people to pool their funds, or join in applying for loans.

If you like the concept of the partnership, but don't like the liability that comes with it, there is a business entity called the Limited Partnership. Although not incorporated, Limited Partnerships must be registered with the Department of State. With a Limited Partnership, there are essentially two classes of partners. First you have the General Partner. This is the person who actually runs the business. When the Limited Partnership is registered with the Department of State, the General Partner must be identified as well. The General Partner has full liability as with any partnership. Then you have Limited Partners. Limited Partners are essentially silent owners. While they have an ownership interest in the business, they have no management authority over the business, and their identity does not need to be revealed in the State filings. And because they have no management authority, they have no liability for activities of the partnership outside their ownership interest. So, like a shareholder their risk is only that their investment in the Limited Partnership could be lost. The general partner however, remains fully liable.

Next you have corporations. A corporation is a separate entity from its owners. Corporations are formed by filing Articles of Incorporation with the Department of State. They are owned by shareholders, managed by Directors and run by officers. The shareholders have no personal liability for the activities of the corporation, outside their investment in the stock.

Finally, you have the Limited Liability Company. This is very similar to a Corporation. It is created by filing Articles of Organization with the Department of State. It is owned by Members, and run by Managers. The Members liability is limited to their investment in the company.

With both corporations and limited liability companies, while the shareholders and members don't have personal liability, neither in most cases do the directors, officers and managers. This is one of the major benefits of corporations and limited liability companies over the limited partnership or general partnerships. Personal liability for the management of the entity is generally limited to intentional wrongdoing. All other liability rests with the entity.

# CORPORATIONS AND LIMITED LIABILITY COMPANIES

**W**hat is the difference between a corporation and a Limited Liability Company? Both are statutory entities, and they have very similar structures. But there are very strong differences between them.

Corporations are governed by Section 607 of the Florida Statutes. They are formed by filing Articles of Incorporation with the Department of State (Sample Articles of Incorporation are attached as Appendix 1). The Articles of Incorporation must set out the name of the company (which must include the words "corporation":, "company" or "incorporated" or the initials "corp.", "co." or "Inc."), the physical and mailing addresses for the company, the name and address of the registered agent (the registered agent must sign the Articles confirming he agrees to serve as the registered agent), the name and addresses of the incorporator, and the number of shares of stock to be issued. The articles may also contain the name and address for the directors and officers of the company, the purpose of the company, and the par value of each share of stock (Par value means the amount paid for each share of stock when it is initially issued).

The main document that controls the actions of the corporation are the Bylaws. These set out details such as when and how meetings are scheduled, how votes are counted, the rights of shareholders, the responsibilities of directors and officers, and financial information such as when dividends are paid. Corporations are owned by Shareholders who generally receive a stock certificate to prove their ownership. Unless the company has a Shareholder's Agreement restricting the transfer of shares, the stock certificates can be freely sold by the shareholders. While many think that shareholders have a lot of power and control, the truth is, their involvement in a company is limited. Shareholders, aside from making an investment in the company and being able to sue if the company acts improperly, only have a say in a couple of areas. The main control aspect is the selection of Directors for the company. Directors are elected by Shareholders at the annual meeting (Corporations are required by law to hold a meeting of the shareholders at least once each year). Shareholders also have the right to vote on certain issues such as when to close down the company or when a company may sell the majority of their assets.

Directors are the long-term planners for a business. They are like the think-tank for the company. The Board of Directors sets out the goals for the company. They also are responsible for selecting the officers of the company.

Officers of a corporation include the President, Vice-President, Secretary and Treasurer. There can be other officers and often there will also be a Chief Executive Officer

(CEO) and Chief Financial Officer (CFO). The officers are responsible for carrying out the instructions of the Directors and running the day-to-day activities of the company.

Limited Liability Companies are very similar to Corporations in structure. There have been major changes recently in the law governing LLCs as the Florida State Legislature completely rewrote the LLC laws in 2014. Today, LLC's are governed by Florida Statute 605 and are formed by filing Articles of Organization with the Department of State (Sample Articles of Organization are attached as Appendix 2). The Articles of Organization must contain the name of the company (which must include the words "Limited Liability Company" or the initials "LLC"), the street and mailing address of the company (these may be the same, but there must be a physical location, not just a P.O. Box), and the name and address of the initial registered agent. The Articles may contain other information, such as whether the company is member managed or manager managed; the name and address of the manager (or one of the members if member-managed), or any special authority of limitation of authority of any person within the company.

Now the concept of member-managed verse manager managed changed greatly with the 2014 revisions. While it was common practice before 2014 to make an LLC member managed and to name one of the members as the manager, with the new legislation, if the LLC is member-managed it means that EVERY member is also a manager. This means that every member has the ability to bind the company, regardless of how great or how little that member's interest is. For this reason, nearly every LLC I form today is deemed Manager-managed. It is also possible not to mention either in the Articles. Rather than give the name of a manager, under the new law, a company can simply list an "authorized person". This is the person with the authority to file the Articles. They do not need to be a member, nor a manager. In this way, the actual ownership and control of the LLC is completely anonymous.

The main document controlling an LLC is the Operating Agreement. Prior to 2014, every LLC was required to have a written Operating Agreement. With the new law, the legislature determined that an Operating Agreement could be in writing or verbal, however if not in writing Courts could determine the terms of the Operating Agreement by looking at the practices if the LLC. LLCs are owned by Members, not shareholders. Instead of stock in a company, Members own membership units and usually receive a membership unit certificate to prove their ownership interest. Before 2014, Membership in an LLC could not be transferred without specific instructions set out in the Articles or Operating Agreement. However, under the 2014 statutes, membership interest is freely transferable, but, the Operating Agreement can put requirements on the process.

Unless the company is member-managed, the Members main job is selecting the Managers. Managers to an LLC are similar to Directors of a Corporation- they handle the long-range planning. LLCs can but are not required to have officers. The Managers can act in their place.

The main differences between corporations and LLCs are in the areas of liability and taxes, which we will cover later.

# CONSIDERATIONS FOR SELECTING A CORPORATION OR LLC

So you've decided to start a new business and you know you want either a corporation or a limited liability company. But what sets them apart? We've already seen that the structure of the two is extremely similar. What makes one really different than the other?

The reason to form either a corporation or limited liability company is to reduce personal liability based on actions of the company. As a general rule, neither shareholders or members have personal liability for issues involving the corporation or LLC. While directors and managers can still have personal liability, so long as they act in a manner consistent with the bylaws or operating agreement and are complying with the law, the liability is also limited. The first major issue to consider are taxes. There are two types of corporations: C corporations and S corporations. The easiest way to think of these are in terms of size; C corporations tend to be large and include most of the publicly traded companies (think McDonalds, IBM, Microsoft and Apple); while S corporations are small with most being mom-and-pop type operations. With a C

Corporation, the corporation must file an annual tax return (due by March 15) and pay income tax based on the profits of the corporation. If the shareholders then receive a dividend based on the profits, they must pay income tax on the dividend. In other words, the shareholders are paying tax twice on the same money. Let's use an example: the Corporation makes $100,000 in profit. If they have a 25% tax bracket, they will pay $25,000 in taxes leaving a profit of $75,000. That $75,000 is then paid to the shareholders as a dividend. If the shareholder is in a 20% tax bracket they will pay an additional $15,000 to the Internal Revenue Service, leaving a net profit of only $60,000 of the original $100,000. That level of taxation is generally too high for small corporations. So to alleviate the impact, Congress created the S corporations (also known as the subchapter S corporation).

Subchapter S corporations have the exact same structure as a C corporation however it must comply with four basic rules: it can have no more than 75 shareholders, all shareholders must be natural persons, the corporation cannot make the majority of its income by investing in other companies (In other words, they should not have subsidiaries, nor invest in other businesses), and the fiscal year must end on December 31. These rules are designed to ensure that S-Corporations remain small businesses. The difference between the S-corporation and a C-Corporation is that an S-corporation pays no income tax. The IRS deems it a nonexistent entity so that all of its profits flow through the corporation directly to the shareholders. In other words using our example above, if the Corporation makes $100,000 in profit, the corporation will file a tax return and issue a k-1 form to the shareholders showing they made $100,000. The shareholders then file their tax return and if they are in the 20% tax bracket, they pay $20,000 in taxes, making a net profit of $80,000.   It is a substantial savings.

However, there is a downside to both types of corporations. Shareholders own stock in the company which is deemed a personal asset.   If the shareholder gets sued personally, the judgment creditor can seize their stock to satisfy the judgment. This means that the creditor can simply take over the business.   This is one of the reasons for the creation of the Limited Liability Company.   But we will discuss that later.

For many businesses, like a personal services corporation, this is not a major issue as the stock has no value without the particular shareholder who owns it. For example, a doctor that has incorporated may be sued, but the stock in his medical practice has little value if he is not there to run it. The value of the company relies on the person who owns it.   But for businesses such as restaurants or retail stores where the company has value on its own merits, a judgment can result in the shareholder losing their business. The creditor can seize their stock and have it sold on the courthouse steps, allowing the creditor to become the owner of the business along with all its assets (including bank accounts).   In order to get around this issue, in 1982 the Florida legislature created the first Limited Liability Company Act. Under the concept of a limited liability company, the owners would not hold shares in a company but rather have membership in an organization. This meant that the ownership interest was protected from a judgment creditor. Just as a judgment creditor could not take away a person's membership in Rotary or The Women's Club, they could not take their membership in an LLC (The judgment creditor could, however, take any dividends the LLC paid to the member. But this new business entity form created tax questions with the IRS. How should an LLC be taxed? Is it a sole proprietorship, a partnership, or a corporation? Initially, they were treated as a partnership, and because of that an LLC had to have more than one member. That view changed with some favorable IRS rulings and the single-member LLC came into existence. The IRS ultimately determined that the owners of an LLC could choose how to be taxed. They can choose to be taxed as a corporation (either C or S) or they can be treated as a disregarded entity where the IRS would ignore the LLC entirely and treat it as a partnership or sole proprietorship. Any member or members would be personally responsible for the taxes (in fact, for a single member LLC choosing to be taxed as a disregarded entity, the LLC does not even need to file a tax return as all income and expense are reported on the member's personal tax return). By default, a single member limited liability company will be treated like a sole proprietorship by the IRS; a multimember limited liability company will be treated like a partnership. The company will only be taxed as a corporation of the LLC actively files for that status. So essentially, by default the LLC receives the income tax benefits of an S-corporation with none of the shareholder liability. In addition, you're not limited to the restrictions of the subchapter S-corporation; i.e. the number of owners is not restricted and the owners do not need to be natural people or US citizens. This allows ownership in an LLC to be held by foreigners and allows the LLC to have subsidiaries. However, if the owners choose to be taxed as a corporation and make the Subchapter S election, they will then need to comply with all of the other requirements for an S-corporation.

Now there are two caveats to this. First is the shareholder liability. In 2012 a judge in Florida determined that a single member LLC was no different than a single member shareholder corporation and for the first time allowed a judgment creditor to seize ownership of a limited liability company. This ruling created controversy throughout the state and was finally addressed by the legislature who crafted a law that essentially states a judgment creditor may not seize the ownership of a limited liability company if the owner can show they will be able to pay off the judgment within a reasonable period of time through the dividends they receive from the company.

The second issue is an increase in tax benefits. Because the IRS allows the owners to determine how they will be taxed, there are additional tax issues to consider. Generally, in a sole proprietorship, partnership, or disregarded entity LLC, all pass-through income is taxed for FICA (self-employment or Social Security tax). However, for LLCs that elect to be taxed like a corporation but then select the subchapter S election, FICA is only charged on the portion of income paid as salary to the owners. In other words, the remaining pass-through money is not subject to this additional tax. If the owner pays themselves a small salary and take the rest of the dividends, they can greatly reduce the tax obligation. These are complicated issues and any businessperson debating what entity to form should consult with their attorney and their accountant to make the selection that works best for them.

# HOW TO FORM A CORPORATION OR LLC

**W**hether you decide to go with a corporation or Limited Liability Company, the formation process is very similar. The first step is to file Articles of Incorporation (corporation) or Articles of Organization (LLC) as was discussed previously. There are a couple of options here. You can draft your own documents and mail them to the Department of State. This process can take a couple of weeks unless you hire a company to walk the papers through the Department. You can also file Articles online through the Department of State's website-www.sunbiz.org. The online system uses a very basic format, but it can result in a corporation being filed in as little as 24-48 hours. The basic information you must include are the name of the company, the physical and mailing addresses, the name and address of the registered agent, and in the case of a corporation, the names of the directors or officers. For Limited Liability Companies, you must list a manager, a member, or an authorized person. By using an authorized person rather than a Member or Manager, the control of the LLC can remain anonymous. One of the persons named in the Articles must sign them.

The name used by the company is important. To

prevent confusion of business identity, only one business entity may use a corporate name. In other words, if I create TREWQ, LLC, no one else in Florida may use that name, regardless of whether they form a corporation or LLC. However, if they make a slight modification, it is allowed. So TREWQ of Key West, Inc. would be permitted. Because of this rule, it is important to check the business name before registering it. To check the name, there are three steps: First on www.sunbiz.org; then click on "Search Records" and then click on "Name". This will let you search every corporate and LLC name registered. If the name is listed, look at the status. If the status is "Active" or "Inact/UA" the name is not available (UA means the company has been dissolved, but by law the name will remain reserved for one year from the date of dissolution, in case the company is reinstated). If the status is "Inact" the name has become available. After clearing the name there, stay in www.sunbiz.org and go to "Search records" and then click on "Trademark Name". While nobody may have registered your proposed business name as a company name, they may have registered it as a trademark. Your use then for a company name might be deemed an infringement. Similarly, once you have cleared the name there, go to www.uspto.gov and click on "Trademarks" and then "Search TESS" to see if your name has been registered as a federal trademark. Once the name is clear on all three databases, you can file your Articles (However, note that while you are conducting your search, someone else may be registering the name, so there is a chance it will still be rejected, requiring you to create a new business name).

There is often confusion over the purpose of the

Registered Agent and Registered Address of a company. Many think the Registered Agent is an officer of the company or a person responsible for running the company, and the Registered Address is the home office. In actuality, the Registered Agent must be a person or business located in Florida, that is available during regular business hours at a specified location (the Registered Address) for the purpose of being served if the company gets sued. They may be a shareholder or member of the company, but do not have to be. As Registered Agent, they have no control over the activities of the company, although they may have authority by virtue of also being an officer or manager. The Registered Agent must sign the Articles of Incorporation or Articles of Organization, certifying that they have read the Registered Agent statute and agree to be bound by its terms.

The other piece of information now required by the Department of State is an email address. While the Department used to send out notices when it was time to renew your company or LLC, to cut costs they began emailing those reminders a few years ago. Nearly all communication with the Department is now done by email.

If filing online, once the Articles are complete and submitted, the Department of State starts processing them. Depending on the workload, this can be done in just a few hours to around three days. Rarely will it take longer than that. Once the processing is complete you will receive an email advising that the company has been registered. This email will include the date and time of the registration, and more importantly provide you with the "Document Number" for the company. This is the number by which your company will be known by the Department. Shortly after you receive the email, you can go to the Department's website (sunbiz.org) and print a copy of your Articles.

# EIN AND SALES TAX NUMBERS

**A**fter you have created your corporation/LLC, the next step is to register the company with the IRS. Unless you are operating the business as a sole proprietorship, before you can do anything with your company, you must get an Employer Identification Number (the exception is a single member LLC which, like a sole proprietorship, may use the owner's social security number).

The Employer Identification Number (EIN) is essentially the social security number for the corporation. It is how the company is known by the IRS. The process to obtain the EIN is pretty straight forward, and can be done by fax, mail or online (If registering a foreign business, you can also register by telephone). While mail will take a couple of weeks and fax will be done in a few days, if you apply online you will get your EIN immediately.

The form to obtain an EIN is IRS Form SS-4. I usually recommend starting with the pdf version which can be found at https://www.irs.gov/pub/irs-pdf/fss4.pdf. A copy of the form can be found at Appendix 7. The online document is a fillable pdf, meaning you can simply fill in the blanks on your computer and save a copy. By completing the pdf form first, you can organize all the information you will need, so you don't get timed out while completing the online version. It also gives you a reference copy for your file. If you allow a third party, such as an attorney or accountant to obtain your EIN, the completion of the pdf version is mandatory as they must possess a signed copy of the SS-4 form before filing for the EIN.

Once the pdf version is complete, you can go to the online application at https://www.irs.gov/businesses/small-businesses-self-employed/apply-for-an-employer-identification-number-ein-online. Whether using the pdf version or the online version, always make sure you are getting the forms from www.IRS.gov. There are a lot of companies that try to look like they are the IRS, but just want to get your money. The IRS does not charge a fee for this service, so if you are asked for a credit card, you are at the wrong site. When you finish the online application, they will give you the Employer Identification Number immediately. Write it down! And print the confirmation page. You will need this number for almost anything you do from this point forward.

With the EIN and your Articles of Organization, you can open a bank account at most financial institutions. If you are going to be selling a product or will be offering a taxable service, you will next need to apply for a sales tax number. This can be obtained from the Florida Department of Revenue at http://floridarevenue.com/taxes/eservices/Pages/registra tion.aspx . You can also download form DR-1N from the Department and mail the completed form, but this process will take several weeks. The online application is a little more in-depth than the EIN application, but if you have a good understanding of your business operations, it should only take about 15 minutes to complete. The end of the application contains several warning statements the applicant MUST acknowledge. These include explanations of the criminal penalties for not filing, filing falsely, or not submitting taxes to the state (Yes, failing to collect, report or remit sales tax is a crime and you can go to jail for it). Because of the importance of these statements, the Sales Tax application must be signed (digitally) by the person making the application or it may be deemed a forgery. As specified in the instructions: "Only the owner of the business or an authorized principal of the business entity may sign this application; an individual granted power of attorney may not sign. The person signing the application must be listed in the Business Structure & Ownership section."

For these purposes, authorized principal generally means an officer of the company; it does not include the company attorney or accountant. When the application is complete, the Department of Revenue will issue you a retrieval code. Write it down! Your sales tax number will not be available for approximately three days. Starting with the third day, you can return to the Department of Revenue website, and by typing in the retrieval code and your EIN (or SSN for sole proprietors or single member LLCs), they will give you the Sales Tax number (It may take longer than three days, so keep checking). About two weeks after the sales tax number is issued, the Department will send you a sales tax certificate and a coupon book for the payment of monthly (or quarterly) tax returns. These certificates must be filed within 20 days of the end of the reporting period. Failure to file within 20 days will subject you to interest and penalties. The first time the report is late, the Department will usually waive the penalties and interest. But that is the only time.

# INSURANCE

There are is no law that requires you to have liability insurance (in most cases); but if you don't, you probably should not be in business. In today's world, insurance is a must. There are too many lawsuits for too many reasons. Even people who are at fault for things such as trespassing have the right to sue for injuries in some circumstances. Without insurance, litigation could bankrupt your business. Most landlords of commercial spaces will require their tenants to have general liability insurance. This is a policy that protects the business in the event someone is injured or something is damaged due to the actions of the business. For example, if someone walks into your store and slips on spilled water, that would be covered by the general liability insurance. Mortgage companies will often require home based businesses to carry liability insurance as well as they do not want the value of the property or the ownership of the property to be placed at risk.

Businesses are often also required by their landlords to have hazard insurance or property and casualty insurance to protect the property and contents from fire or other harm. Similarly, they may require flood and windstorm insurance. Landlords often also require plate glass insurance to protect large picture windows from damage.

Businesses that have employees generally must carry workman's compensation insurance. For most business this is not required unless they have at least four (4) employees, although agricultural businesses do not need it until they have six (6) employees while the construction industry must have worker's compensation if they have just one (1) employee (For construction companies, workman's compensation insurance can be waived if the only employees are officers of the company who own at least 10% of the company).

Any business reliant on automobiles must have automobile insurance. Your personal automobile insurance will not cover the car if it is used primarily for business purposes. This includes rideshare services.

The above insurance policies protect the business for injuries to others, to workers, or to the property itself. However, there are two types of insurance to protect the business in the event of harm to the company. The first is business interruption insurance. This protects the income stream of the business after a disaster or covered risk temporarily stops the business from operating. This insurance can cover the expenses of the business as well as provide for the profits the business would have made during the period it is shut down. This can be substantial if a building is destroyed and must be rebuilt before the business can be restarted.

The other policy is key man insurance. This is essentially a life/disability insurance policy taken out by the company to cover anyone the company deems important to carry out the functions of the company. This policy covers hiring and training a replacement, lost sales, losses covered by the extended absence of the key person, covers guarantees the key person may have signed, and even shareholder buy-out requirements.

The company should also consider Directors/Officers insurance (referred to as D&O Insurance). This is a policy that protects the directors and officers of a company in the event they get sued for actions they take on behalf of the company. The policy can cover defense costs for criminal, administrative and civil litigation, as well as damages. It generally will not protect the directors and officers from intentional illegal acts.

Finally, for professionals such as attorneys, physicians, architects, and accountants there is professional liability insurance. This is often referred to as malpractice insurance, however, that phrase implies wrongdoing. While professional liability insurance covers malpractice actions, it also provides coverage when the professional did everything right but is being sued anyway.

# COMPANY RECORDS

There are some housekeeping matters to address once you have started your new company. Whether it is a corporation or LLC, it is recommended that you obtain a corporate book. This is simply a notebook that contains all of your corporate documents. If you purchase it through a business records supply house, it will include your corporate seal, stock or membership certificates and pre-printed forms for your initial start-up. You don't have to have all of this; the corporate seal and certificates are generally optional. But by law, business entities MUST retain certain records. For corporations they must keep the following:

- The Articles of Incorporation and any amendments
- Bylaws or restated bylaws and any amendments
- Minutes of all meetings of directors and shareholders for the last three years
- Resolutions adopted by the board of directors creating one or more classes or series of shares and their relative rights, preferences and limitations
- A record of all actions taken by shareholders or directors without a meeting for the last three years
- A record of all actions taken by a committee of the board of directors in place of the board of directors
- All written communications to shareholders for the past three years

• A record of shareholders listed alphabetically and by series of shares held by each
• A list of names and business addresses of the current directors and officers
• The corporation's most recent annual report

For Limited Liability Companies, the list is slightly different:

• A copy of the articles of organization, articles of merger, articles of interest exchange, articles of conversion, and articles of domestication, and other documents and all amendments thereto, concerning the limited liability company which were filed with the department, together with executed copies of any powers of attorney pursuant to which any articles of organization or such other documents were executed.
• A copy of the then-effective operating agreement, if made in a record, and all amendments thereto if made in a record.
• A current list of the full names and last known business, residence, or mailing addresses of each member and manager.
• Copies of the limited liability company's federal, state, and local income tax returns and reports, if any, for the 3 most recent years.
• Copies of the financial statements of the limited liability company, if any, for the 3 most recent years.
• Unless contained in an operating agreement made in a record, a record stating the amount of cash and a description and statement of the agreed value of the property or other benefits contributed and agreed to be contributed by each member, and the times at which or

occurrence of events upon which additional contributions agreed to be made by each member are to be made.

The corporate book gives a convenient location to retain these records to ensure they are protected and don't get misplaced in the event they are needed.

The book can also be used to house your insurance records, leases and any other corporate record that you may need to reference occasionally.

# OPERATING AGREEMENTS VS BYLAWS AND SHAREHOLDER AGREEMENTS

If you have formed a corporation or LLC, you need to consider how they will be managed or run. Running a company is different than running a business, which means if you have formed a company to run your business, you will have twice the work.

Organizing the company starts with planning (Again). For a corporation, organizing is done through Bylaws and Shareholder Agreements. For LLC's it is through the Operating Agreement.

The Florida Statutes give little instruction for bylaws. All it states is that the bylaws may contain any provision for managing the business and regulating the affairs of the corporation that is not inconsistent with law or the articles of incorporation. Usually, they will contain provisions for scheduling meetings, voting rights, duties of directors and officers, shareholder status, and maintenance of the corporation (Sample ByLaws are attached as Appendix 3).

They are generally fairly short, so they are often supplemented with a Shareholders Agreement.

A Shareholders Agreement is a contract between the shareholders as to each other and between the shareholders and the company (A sample Shareholder's Agreement is attached as Appendix 4). Because it falls under contract law rather than corporate law, it allows for more flexibility and privacy. These agreements set out the rights of shareholders to buy and sell their shares of the company, and can include things such as valuation, control, and can even discuss issues such as continuing shareholder obligations.

For an LLC, the Operating Agreement essentially does the job of both the Bylaws and the Shareholders Agreement. The statutes give more instruction for Operating Agreements than Bylaws. Before 2014, written Operating Agreements were mandatory, however the law has been changed to state that while an LLC must have an operating agreement, it may be verbal, written or implied. The Operating Agreement is to include discussions of the relation between members as to each other and the LLC, the rights and duties of the manager; the activities and affairs of the company and the conduct of those activities and affairs; and the means and conditions for amending the operating agreement. It may not do any of the following: Vary a limited liability company's capacity to sue and be sued in its own name; Vary the governing law over the LLC; vary the requirement, procedure, or other provisions pertaining to registered agents; eliminate the duty of loyalty or the duty of care; eliminate the obligation of good faith and fair dealing; relieve or exonerate a person from liability for conduct involving bad faith, willful or intentional misconduct, or a knowing violation of law; unreasonably restrict the duties and rights regarding availability of records by members and managers; vary the grounds for dissolution; vary the requirement to wind up the company's business, activities, unreasonably restrict the right of a member to maintain a derivative action against the company, vary the right of a member to approve a merger, interest exchange, or conversion, vary the required contents of plan of merger, or provide for indemnification for a member or manager for any of the following: Conduct involving bad faith, willful or intentional misconduct, or a knowing violation of law, A transaction from which the member or manager derived an improper personal benefit, liability for an improper distribution, or a breach of duties loyalty and care.

The Operating Agreement may also specify penalties for members and managers who fail to comply with the terms of the Operating Agreement (A sample Operating Agreement is attached as Appendix 5).

These documents are the controlling records for the company. If drafted too tightly or too loosely, they can lead to unwanted litigation. For this reason, it is not recommended that they be drafted without the help of an attorney well versed in business law.

# SALES TAX

**E**very new business needs to consider their tax liability. While there are numerous types of taxes (real estate tax, tangible property tax, self- employment tax, etc.), probably the most frequent, and sometimes the most confusing, is the sales tax. Why is this tax confusing? Well, not everything is taxed, not every county taxes the same amount and not everything even in the same County is taxed at the same level.

What is taxed? Generally, the retail sale of merchandise is taxable, while the providing of services is not. However, that is a gross oversimplification. Not all retail sales are taxed, and not all services are untaxed. Most food is not taxed. However, heated or prepared food, food sold for on-premises consumption, soda and soft drinks (including fruit drinks), alcoholic beverages and candy are all taxable. Many medicines and home based medical diagnosis kits, as well as many home remedies are not taxable. Prosthetics and orthopedic equipment, optical equipment and most feminine hygiene products are exempt. However, toiletries are generally not exempt. Generally, sales made within the state are taxable, but sales that are shipped to other states are not. As to services, most services are not taxable; however, commercial pest control services, nonresidential cleaning services, commercial security services and detective services are all taxable, as are certain contractors who sell tangible property with their contracting services. Also the leasing of commercial property is taxable, although leasing nontransient residential real estate is not (For sales tax purposes, nontransient means any lease of six months or less). In addition to the above exemptions, Florida also has a sales tax holiday. Usually in August of each year, there is a weekend set out where the purchase of clothes, computers and school supplies are not taxed. This is to assist families who need to prepare their children for school.

The State Sales Tax rate is normally 6%. However, starting 2018, the sales tax amount for leases of commercial real estate was reduced to 5.8%. On top of the State sales tax, each county is authorized to add a discretionary sales surtax. These vary by county. In Monroe County, the surtax rate is currently 1.5%. So the general sales tax rate in Monroe County would be 7.5% for most items, and 7.3% for commercial real estate leases.

This mix of taxable and non-taxable, and varying rates is confusing and as mentioned above, failure to collect and remit tax can be criminal, so you don't want to get this wrong. Discuss your business with an accountant so you are clear what charges are taxable and what are not. If you do not have an accountant (and as a business owner, you should), you can call the Department of Revenue and they will advise you if the item is taxable or not.

# LOCAL OCCUPATIONAL LICENSE

**P**rior to opening a new business must obtain a local occupational license, sometimes referred to as a business tax application. While the state does not issue occupational licenses, cities and counties do. If your business is located in an unincorporated area, you will need a County license; if located in a city, you will need both a City license and a County license (generally, you apply for the city license first, and then for your County license. The County usually will confirm with the city that their license has been issued before granting the County license). In the situation where the business is strictly online, it will be deemed to be located where the primary office or mailing address is located. Even online businesses must obtain a local occupational license.

Because getting the occupational license is essentially the last step to opening a business, you should be almost ready to start operations when applying. For a corporation or limited liability company, the company must be registered with the Department of State before applying for your local license. All businesses must have an Employer Identification Number, except for sole proprietorship's or single member limited liability companies which may simply use the owner's Social Security number. If operating under a business name different than the owner's name or the company name, a fictitious name application must be registered with the Department of State before applying for your local business tax license. The clerk's office will usually confirm the registration online before granting a license. In some cases, you will also need your sales tax number.

The requirements for local occupational licenses vary based on the type of business you're opening. Generally, every business will need a copy of a deed showing they own the property where the business is located, a commercial lease showing they are authorized to do business at that location, or a residential lease along with a letter from the landlord authorizing the operation of the business out of the property. In all situations, the property must be appropriately zoned for that type of business.

In addition, any other license or permit that is required for the business must be obtained before getting an occupational license. For example, a restaurant will need a fire inspection as well as authorization from the Department of Health or Department of Business and Professional Regulation. A state registered business such as a cosmetologist must first have their state license. A professional office such as attorney or doctor must have a copy of their professional license. If the license is for a professional business such as a law firm or architectural firm, each individual professional within that firm must have their own occupational license. If the license is for a business such as a barbershop or salon where the employees receive a salary and commission, the individuals do not need a separate license. However, if the salon requires the individual to lease a chair within the salon, they do need a separate license.

Some businesses may qualify for a home occupational license, but this usually requires that a floor plan of the building be submitted designating what portion of the home will be used for the business (there is a limitation on how much of a home may be used).

Once issued, the local occupational license must be renewed every year.

# COMMERCIAL LEASES

**B**efore applying for an occupational license, a business must have a location to work out of. Unless the business owner owns the location, they will need to obtain a lease. For a home based business, this may simply be a residential lease with a letter of authorization from the landlord, but for the vast majority of businesses, they will need a commercial lease.

Commercial leases vary substantially from residential leases. Often residential leases are verbal, while almost all commercial leases are written. While residential leases are often fairly short, commercial leases tend to be lengthy. Residential leases are rarely longer than one year; most commercial leases are for several years. Most provisions of a residential lease are covered by the Florida statutes; most provisions of a commercial lease are covered by the lease itself. Where the landlord has primary maintenance responsibilities for most residential leases, in commercial leases, most maintenance issues are transferred to the tenant. Often commercial leases also transfer the landlord's insurance cost, property taxes and general maintenance expenses directly to the tenant. In addition, while most residential rent is not taxable, commercial rent is taxable.

*Basics of Starting a Florida Business*

In addition to rent and security deposits, some landlords require key money just to get into a commercial unit and also charge an additional fee for "common area maintenance" or CAM. In some leases, the landlord also adds in an administrative fee on top of all of these expenses. For example a lease can require the tenant to pay the landlords property taxes along with a 15% administrative fee to cover the landlord's costs of processing the tax payment. Finally, there are leases that require the Tenant to report their sales to the Landlord, and in some cases, even pay a portion of their profits to the landlord as additional rent. Therefore, when planning the operating expenses for a business, the business owner must take into account not just the rent, but all the additional charges associated with the commercial lease.

Many commercial tenants, especially new business owners, do not anticipate the potential maintenance issues that may arise. Depending on the lease, these may be as little as maintaining the interior of their store or may be as great as covering repairs to the structural components of the building. This means that if there is a crack in the foundation of the building or a leak in the roof, the tenant may be responsible for the full cost of repairing that item, even if there is relatively little time left on their lease.

The tenant must also consider the length of the lease. While a short lease gives the tenant protection in the event the business fails, a longer lease gives them security of rent control if the business is successful.

The tenant needs to also carefully review the provision of the lease regarding the sale of the business. While some leases freely allow tenants to sell the business, often the sale of the business requires the landlord's approval and in some cases the landlord will require payment of administrative expenses to review the proposed sale or even demand a portion of the sale price be paid to the landlord.

If the property is going to need preparation to accommodate the tenant, such as installation of floor coverings, cabinets, etc., the tenant can request a buildout period. This is a period of time during which no rent is paid so that the tenant can do all the construction necessary to open the business.

While all aspects of a commercial lease are important, probably the section to pay closest attention to is the default section. While any violation of the lease can be deemed a breach, the default section tells you when a violation is deemed a breach of the lease and what the remedies for that breach are. Most of the time these clauses are fairly standard, with a few modifications on timing. Unlike residential leases where the statutes are controlling, in commercial leases, the terms of the lease control (usually).

The most common breach is not paying the rent on time. If rent is due on the first, it needs to be paid on the first. Some lease will give a grace period; others will not. Most leases allow the landlord to give the tenant a written notice the day after the rent is due demanding the tenant to either pay the rent or leave the property. Most of the time, the Tenant is given three days, but occasionally it is longer. During that period, if the tenant tries to pay the rent, the landlord must accept it. After the deadline, the landlord is entitled to evict the tenant.

Most leases state that if the tenant violates the lease in a way other than failing to paying rent, such as failing to make repairs, failing to pay utility bills, or subleasing the property, the Landlord must give the tenant a notice specifying what the violation is. If it is a minor violation, the tenant should be given time to fix whatever the violation is. Usually this is a seven day period. However, if the violation is one that puts the property at risk or puts people in harm's way (examples would include demolition work within the unit, harassment or acts of violence towards anyone, or unsafe working conditions), the landlord does not need to give the tenant an opportunity to fix the violation- they can just give them notice that they must leave. This is usually a seven day notice as well. These notices are generally mandatory (although rare, I have seen leases that do not require advance notices and in commercial leases, there have been cases where the "no notice provision" was allowed).

Equally as important as the notice provision is the remedy provision. What can the landlord do after the breach has been determined. Most leases have a combination of clauses. Once the tenant has been evicted, the landlord can ask the court to order the tenant to pay rent each month as it comes due until the landlord finds a new tenant, or the Court can order the tenant to pay all the rent that would have been due under the lease if it had gone to its natural conclusion. In other words, if there is still three years left on the lease, the court can order the tenant to pay three years rent immediately. The court can also simply give the landlord possession so he can re-rent the property or even use it for his own purposes. If the violation is something other than nonpayment of rent, the landlord can fix the violation and then charge the tenant for the cost. Many leases allow the landlord to simply come in and take over the property without court action. These clauses are not enforceable. Florida has a strict law that requires all evictions to be done through the Court. This means self-help evictions are not allowed (Landlords are however able to retake possession when tenants have abandoned or surrendered the property).

# DESIGNING YOUR STORE

**O**nce you have your lease in place and are ready to start designing the layout of your store, you may want to consider consulting an architect, attorney or interior designer. Planning the interior (and in some cases, the exterior) of your business includes many legal considerations. In 1990, Congress passed the Americans With Disabilities Act (the ADA) which mandates that all businesses open to the public provide access to those with disabilities. What does that mean? While planning your business, you must consider all aspects of the business to ensure that all people have the same level of access to all parts of the building. This includes not just customers, but employees, so your plans need to include both the front of the house and the back of the house, to use a restaurant phrase.

Approximately 19% of our population has a disability. For some their disability affects mobility; for some it affects perception; for some communication. A business location involves all of these. Mobility impacts how people get in, out and around a store. Perception involves how people understand what is happening within the store. Communication involves how people interact with the store. If you break any of these three, you lose a customer. If a customer can't get in the store, if they don't know what you're selling, or if they can't tell your employees what they want, they can't buy your goods.

The ADA puts certain requirements on businesses to break down the barriers that keep those with disabilities from enjoying the same benefits as those without. It is a laudable goal. But in some cases, the requirements are so detailed that the average business owner cannot follow them without professional help. Let's look at a few examples. We will use a retail store as this most effectively shows the impacts that can occur.

We start outside the store. Can a person in a wheelchair get from your parking lot to the front door? Are there curbs they have to get over? Are there stairs they have to go up? If so, it is possible that the curbs need to be removed or a ramp built to provide access around the stairs. If you wish to install a ramp, is it going to be wide enough (Under the ADA it must be at least 36 inches wide with a 5'x5' platform at the top and bottom of the ramp). Once at the front door, is the doorway wide enough for a wheelchair to get through? Doors must have 32 inches of clear space. Is it a heavy door? It cannot require more than 5lbs of force to open. Is there a threshold? It cannot be more than half an inch high, unless properly beveled. How about clearance to open the door? Well that depends on if it swings in or out. How about the aisles of the store? Aisles should be 36 inches wide with room to make a turn at the end if necessary. If the store is too small to make all aisles sufficiently wide, or if merchandise is displayed too high, the store can accommodate this by having sufficient staff on hand to retrieve merchandise for those who cannot reach it.

Is there a bathroom in the store? The toilet needs to be 17-19 inches tall and 16-18 inches from the center to the wall. The sink should be no more than 34 inches high, and between 11 and 25 inches deep. The bottom edge of the mirror should be no higher than 40 inches. And there must be at least enough room for a circle with a 60-inch diameter for a wheelchair to turn around. Do you accept credit cards? If so, you need to ensure that there is a counter area no more than 36 inches high and at least 36 inches long for wheelchair customers to sign slips. Do you allow service animals and have staff to help customers with visual disabilities? You should. If serving food, how many accessible tables do you have? One is required with 27 inches of knee space and a table height of between 28 and 34 inches. These are just a fraction of the ADA rules regarding store layout.

As honorable as the goal of the ADA is, enforcement is anything but. The law allows for any person who is precluded from visiting the store due to lack of ADA accessibility to file suit against the business, without giving the business prior notice and an opportunity to cure. Offending businesses not only have to come into compliance, but the also have to pay damages and legal fees. The cost of an ADA suit can easily be in the tens of thousands of dollars, and in extreme cases can exceed $100,000. There is an old phrased that an ounce of prevention is worth a pound of cure. That applies here. The cost of getting a professional to make sure you are in compliance is far less than the cost of coming into compliance because of a lawsuit.

# HIRING

There are full semester classes just on labor law and entire books on hiring. There is no way I can cover everything in this primer. But I can give you an overview.

First you have to find potential employees. There are numerous ways to do this: you can put ads in newspapers or online, post job notices, use word of mouth or hire an employment agency. However, you need to do this in a fair method that does not discriminate against a certain group. Job postings must be neutral and not discourage certain groups from applying. For example, if the posting looks for "recent college graduates", it may discriminate against the elderly. If word-of-mouth is primarily among white workers, it may discriminate against minorities.

If you want to avoid all the hiring requirements, you can find workers through an employee leasing company. These are businesses that do the hiring and then lease their employees to other businesses. The leasing companies charge the business and then pay their employees, handling all tax filings and paperwork.

If you hire employees on your own, you will need to interview them to make sure they are a good fit for your business. There are a number of different interview styles employers use. Some prefer a one-on-one interview, some have a panel interviewing the applicants. Interviews can be in person, by phone or even skype. Some even do a written interview, however, this is usually not recommended as you do not get to see the applicant while they are responding and don't know what resources they are using while responding. Some interviewers like to hold the interview over lunch or dinner so they can watch the applicant's behavior in an informal setting (I read of one interviewer who always held the interview over lunch to see if the applicant reached for salt before tasting the food. That was a sign that the applicant acted without researching).

Regardless of the interview style, the interview process is fraught with risks, so you will need to know what you can ask and what you cannot. There are laws that restrict what you can ask. Violating these rules can subject the employer to charges of discrimination. The interview should be based on determining the applicant's ability to do the job. Do they have the proper qualifications? Do they have the ability to do the job? Make sure all questions are job-relevant.

Some questions are clearly off limits. You cannot ask any questions regarding race. It is improper to ask an applicant about disabilities, other than to ask if they can perform the essential job functions, either with or without reasonable accommodations. You may ask them to demonstrate their ability to perform the job function. An employer cannot ask an applicant their age, except to provide proof they are over 18 years old. You may not ask an applicant about their religious beliefs, but you can ask if they can work on Saturday or Sunday if the job requires it. Questions that seem innocuous or irrelevant can be illegal.

Seemingly neutral questions can illicit improper information. It is improper to ask an applicant about their membership in any club, social organization, or union membership. You can, however, ask about membership in a relevant professional association. Employers cannot ask the applicant if they are married or have children. The employer may not ask if an applicant has been arrested, but they can ask if the applicant has ever been convicted of a crime. It is improper to ask about alcohol use, although it is permissible to ask if the applicant is currently using illegal drugs.

If the applicant volunteers information that the employer is not allowed to ask about, the best practice is to not follow up on that information and not to write anything down regarding that information. These rules are in place to protect the employee from discrimination, and the employer from claims of discrimination. Employment decisions cannot be based at all upon improper information.

To better protect themselves, employers should put together a structured interview so that every applicant is asked the same set of questions.

Once an employer is satisfied with the answers the prospective employee gives, it is time to make an offer of employment. This can be an outright offer where the employee accepts and starts working. However, if the employer wants to seek more information, they can give the employee a conditional letter of employment. This is a written offer of employment that sets out all the terms of the job- the position, the pay, the starting date. It should also state that the job is contingent on completion of certain conditions. If the conditions are not satisfactorily met, the offer is rescinded. Generally, background checks, drug tests and criminal records should not be requested until a conditional letter of employment is issued.

Once you have decided who to hire, they must complete two forms: the W-4 withholding allowance and the I-9 Verification of Citizenship. The W-4 is available from the IRS and the I-9 is available from the U.S. Citizenship and Immigration Services. The I-9 is not submitted to the Immigration Office, but the employer must have one for every employment and keep it on file for three years. The employer must also register with the Department of Revenue to file unemployment tax (this should have been done when the business applied for their EIN, but if not, they need to register before their first payroll is completed) and, depending on the number of employees, obtain workman's compensation insurance. There are also a series of posters you must display inside the workplace as required by the US Department of Labor.

Each employee should have a separate file and if the employer obtains any medical information on the employee as part of the background information, that information should be in a separate file kept in a locked cabinet.

# EMPLOYEES VS. INDEPENDENT CONTRACTORS

**A**s part of the hiring process, the employer needs to determine if they want to hire employees or independent contractors. An independent contractor is not an employee of the business; they work for themselves and are hired by the employer to perform a specific task. That task may be a small project, or it can be a continuing activity, taking months or years. Many times, independent contractors can look very similar to employees. There are benefits to using independent contractors, but there are penalties if you misclassify them.

For employees, the employer must pay a portion of social security, Medicare and unemployment compensation, as well as workman's compensation. These expenses are not required when using independent contractors. Similarly, if the business offers benefits to its employees such as sick leave, vacation and retirement, these benefits do not transfer to the independent contractor. Independent contractors do not have the right to unionize, and do not have the same rights against certain types of discrimination and may not be covered under minimum wage/overtime laws. Finally, the independent contractors job is done when the task is complete, so there is no need to fire them and no risk of a claim for unemployment compensation.

On the other hand, the employer has less control over an independent contractor. Because they are being hired for a task, the goal of the employer is the end, not the means. The independent contractor has more autonomy to determine how best to accomplish the goal. The independent contractor generally has the right to hire his own workers, meaning you may have people working for you that you do not know. Because they are not covered by workman's compensation, if an independent contractor gets hurt on the job, the employer may be fully responsible for his injuries. Also, any intellectual property created by the independent contractor, such as artwork, writings, plans, etc. belong to the independent contractor; whereas any such item created by an employee is owned by the employer. Finally, independent contractors are not favored by the IRS. The government makes less money from independent contractors, so they may audit the business if they believe the position is misclassified.

Because of the financial benefits, many employers will try to classify all of their workers as independent contractors. Truthfully, though, most workers are more properly classified as employees. It is difficult sometimes to determine which is which. There is no bright line test to determine if a worker is an independent contractor or an employee. Previously, the IRS had a twenty-point checklist that was reviewed to determine if a worker was an employee or an independent contractor. Now, they look at three items:

- Behavioral: Does the company control or have the right to control what the worker does and how the worker does his or her job?
- Financial: Are the business aspects of the worker's job controlled by the payer? (these include things like how worker is paid, whether expenses are reimbursed, who provides tools/supplies, etc.)
- Type of Relationship: Are there written contracts or employee type benefits (i.e. pension plan, insurance, vacation pay, etc.)? Will the relationship continue and is the work performed a key aspect of the business?

These are not always clear, so the twenty-point test can still be reviewed to help clarify the position. The reason this test is based on the IRS rulings is that the issue often comes up during an IRS audit. However, the issue can also arise from a review by a state agency or if a worker sues for benefits that are withheld. Often these lawsuits end up being class-action suits that can cost the employer millions (In 2007, FedEx settled a mislabeling suit for $228 million; in 2014, Lowe's settled a suit for $6.5 million; in 2016 Uber settled a suit for $68 million). If the IRS determines that the business has misclassified the workers as independent contractors, the penalties can be severe. The business can be ordered to pay all employment related taxes that would have been due for that employee. They can also be ordered to give the worker all benefits that the worker should have received during their time with the business. In one of the most well-known cases, the IRS audited

Microsoft and determined that in 1989-90, Microsoft had mislabeled numerous employees. In that case, Microsoft had employed hundreds of workers and had each sign a contract stating they were independent contractors and had no rights to any benefits Microsoft gave to its regular employees, such as stock options, retirement benefits, etc. The workers were paid through accounts payable instead of payroll and were responsible for their own insurance. Most of these workers wanted to be classified as independent contractors and were actually paid more than if they had been employees. So, the workers were happy and Microsoft was happy. But the IRS was not happy. The IRS contended these were actually employees. After years in court it was determined that some 8,000-12,000 misclassified workers were in fact employees. Microsoft reclassified some as employees; some were transferred to a temporary employment company and some were let go. They also had to pay substantial penalties. But that wasn't the end. The newly reclassified workers then sued, claiming that since they were employees all along, they should be granted all the benefits they should have received from the day of employment. The Court agreed, and Microsoft had to give all the workers stock options and to allow the workers to participate in a 401(k) matching program going back to when the workers first began. The ultimate cost was in excess of $100 million.

The IRS does allow the businesses some protections. If the business is not sure how to classify their employees, they can ask the IRS to review the position and determine what the classification should be. This process can take as long as six months. In addition, a business that has been misclassifying their employees can do a voluntary reclassification for future work. This provides those businesses with relief from the penalties of misclassification.

# INTELLECTUAL PROPERTY

**E**arlier in this book I briefly mentioned intellectual property. There are four basic types of Intellectual Property. Three are protectable, one is not. The three protectable forms are copyrights, patents and trademarks. The one form that is not protectable is trade secrets. Actually, to say that trade secrets are not protectable is a bit of a misnomer. Trade secrets are protectable to the extent they are exposed between persons with a confidential relationship.

A trade secret is just that: a secret. It is essentially business know how that is not known by your competitors. It consists of anything the business has developed that they protect from outside knowledge. Trade secrets should be on a need to know basis and those employees who know the trade secrets should be required to sign non-disclosure agreements. If the business takes steps to keep the secrets confidential and the secret gets in the hands of a competitor, the business can get a court order preventing the competitor from using the trade secret. However, if the business does not take sufficient steps to protect the secret, the competitors have the right to use it. As an example, several years ago two employees of Coca Cola tried to sell trade secrets about New Coke to it's rival Pepsi.

Luckily, Pepsi knew the law and contacted Coke to advise them what was happening. A sting was set up and the two employees were caught red-handed (a small trademark pun for those who caught it) and were ultimately sentenced to between 5 and 8 years in prison plus restitution of over $40,000.

A copyright is the protection of an artistic creation. It is the legal ability of an author, artist or composer to protect his creation from being reproduced, performed, or disseminated without permission. The copyright holder also has the right to prepare derivative works, sell or lend copies to the public, to perform works before the public for profit, and to display the works. Originally, copyrights were designed to protect "writings". Now, however, it protects any "original work of authorship fixed in any tangible medium of expression". The first requirement is that the work be original. This means that it must be the applicant's creation. The item must be non-utilitarian, in other words, the item cannot have its design merely because of its useful considerations. (This might however allow for patent protection). Finally, it must be fixed. A mere idea or method of operation is not copyrightable. Also, an impromptu speech or live performance that are not recorded cannot be copyrighted.

The statute specifies a number of types of works. Specifically, it grants protection to:

Literary works-this includes any written work such as books, articles, and essays. It also includes items such as computer programs, written speeches, catalogs, and advertising.

Musical works, including any accompanying words-

This covers both the written music and the lyrics.

Dramatic works, including any accompanying music- Plays, operas, musicals are covered including any songs that are part of the play.

Pantomimes and choreographic works- written or recorded dances, steps, or actions.

Pictorial, graphic, and sculptural works- This includes sketches, paintings, photographs, greeting cards, blueprints, maps, statues, jewelry, models, fabric patterns, and wallpaper.

Motion pictures and other audiovisual works- Movies, videotapes, filmstrips.

Sound recordings- This includes recordings of songs, voices and sound effects.

In 1984, Congress expanded copyright protection to semi-conductor chips. The copyright statute also allows protection for compilations. That is, collections of existing materials can be copyrighted as a whole. This also includes lists. As an example, the telephone book could be copyrighted as a list of names and phone numbers. Many phone books have traps printed in them to catch would be infringers. For example, I have seen Barney and Betty Rubble listed in the phone book, or Fred and Wilma Flintstone. If these names and numbers appear on someone else's phone book, it is proof of copying.

Finally, the statute allows for protection of derivative works. The most famous example of this is a photograph of a painting. The photograph is a derivation of the original and is itself copyrightable. Translations are derivations as well and thus are copyrightable. The copyright holder has the right to control these derivations.

Certain items specifically cannot be copyrighted. They include items not yet fixed in tangible form (mere ideas), titles, names, slogans, procedures, ingredients (although a recipe may be copyrighted), blank forms, government documents (such as those at the back of this book), buildings, typefaces, and common information such as calendars. Finally, trademarks, no matter how creative, cannot be copyrighted.

Registering a copyright is a fairly simple process. The application is filed online at www.copyright.gov. The filing fee is only $35. A copy of the copyrighted item- either the actual text or a photograph of the artwork, must accompany the application. Although the application is simple, the process will take several months. An infringement lawsuit cannot be filed until the registration is complete and for those infringements that occur before registration, the copyright owner can only get injunctive relief- no damages and no fees and costs. Once registered the copyright last for the life of the owner plus 95 years, or when owned by a corporation, it lasts 125 years from the date of creation.

A trademark is the right to use a word, name, symbol, design or combination of these to identify goods and distinguish them from goods made by others. The use of symbols or words to identify services such as restaurants are called "service marks" but follow the same rules as trademarks.

A trademark may be federal, state, or common law. A federal trademark protects the mark throughout the United States; a state trademark protects the mark through the state and a common-law trademark protects the mark within the businesses immediate market area. Because a common-law trademark is not registered, in the event of infringement, the owner can only get an injunction preventing further infringement- but no damages, fees or costs. The reasons for trademark protection is to identify the source of goods or services, so a buyer can be assured of the quality of the goods or services.

Trademarks are also limited as to what is covered, but again, the list is liberal. Trademark protection has been granted to colors, composites, labels, letters, musical notes, names, numerals, packaging, symbols, words and phrases. Examples of trademarks include: IBM, 7-UP, Wendy's, the green stripe on Burlington socks, the label of a soup can, the shape of Coke bottles, the NBC musical notes, McDonald's golden arches, the color pink for insulation, etc.

Like with copyrights, there are certain items that cannot be given full trademark protection. These include purely generic names, immoral, deceptive or scandalous names, flags or insignia of any country, the name portrait or signature of a living person without their consent, the name, portrait or signature of any deceased President of the United States during the lifetime of his widow, a mark which is primarily geographic, or a mark which is confusingly similar to an unabandoned or registered mark. There are, however, methods in which to protect some of these items to a lesser level.

Every State has their own trademark registration process and they are usually easier, faster and cheaper than a federal application. For a federal trademark, the application is found at www.uspto.gov. The filing fee is

$325 per mark per class (The fee can be reduced if the filing meets certain criteria).   Now let me explain "per mark per class".   Per mark means if you have a name and logo, you can file an application for the name and logo together, just the name, and/or just the logo. That would be up to three marks.   Per class is more confusing. There are around 45 classes of trademarks. For example, clothing is a class; glassware is a class; food items are a class, alcoholic beverages are a class, nonalcoholic beverages are a class; paint is a class, entertainment services are a class; business services are a class.   For each class there is an additional filing fee.   So, if you have two marks in three classes, the fee would be $325 x 6=$1,950 (unless you qualify for the lower filing fee-usually $275 per mark per class).   The process is not quick.   It takes easily eight months to process an application and that time can increase to up to two years.   While a business owner can complete the application process on their own, it is a nuanced application and a mistake will lead to a rejection of the mark.   Indeed, the majority of trademark applications are rejected on their first review.   It is recommended that the business owner considers hiring an attorney with experience processing trademark applications.

Certain activities are not affected by trademark protection.   For example, a trademark will not prevent a prior user from continuing to use the infringing mark in the same locale it has been used in the past.   Trademark also does not cover any items except those listed in the class stated in the application.   In other words, if you have received a trademark for clothing, another person will be able to use the same mark for medicines or furniture.

Trademarks can also be used by a competitor to compare items in advertising. Finally, the owner of an item may use the trademark of that item to sell it (example-a person may advertise the brand of his car when trying to sell the car).

Once the trademark is in use, the business can prevent any other business from using a mark that is the same or so similar as to create customer confusion. If the average person would see the two marks and be confused as to whether they come from the same source, there is infringement. Trademark protection initially lasts 10 years, but must be affirmed between the fifth and sixth year and again in the tenth year. It is then renewed every 10 years.

A patent is a protection given to inventors for items, designs, and life forms (Some of these items may also be subject to copyright protection). Unless the business is based on an invention, or if the business owner has developed a unique process, patent application is not something normally considered in starting a business. Patents are extremely complicated, requiring research and detailed drawings. Generally, they should not be applied for by the lay person without the assistance of a patent attorney. Patent attorneys are different from non-patent attorneys. To be patent certified, the attorney must have a science or engineering background and must pass a special patent bar examination. If they do not meet the qualifications, they are precluded from processing a patent application. Patents last for 15 years from registration.

When starting a new business, the owner needs to consider protecting their intellectual property. The company creates a business name- that is a trademark. You have an employee manual-that is a copyright. These are business assets and can make the business more valuable if you register them.

If the business wants to protect their intellectual property, a little planning is necessary. If the item is created by an employee, the intellectual property is owned by the business. If, however, it is created by an independent contractor or a third party such as a graphic artist, the contractor or artist owns the intellectual property. For this reason, it is important that, when hiring a third party to create a trademark or copyright item, the agreement should include a written provision that the third party will assign all their rights to the item to the business.

If there is an infringement of a copyright or trademark remedies are provided through the Courts. This is the one area where copyright and trademarks are the same. Both have four basic forms of relief from infringements. First is injunctive relief. If the court finds infringement of either a copyright or trademark, they may permanently restrain the other person from further use of the item or mark.

Second is monetary damages. A copyright infringer can be ordered to pay actual damages (the amount of money the copyright holder actually lost due to the infringement). The amount can also be based on the profit made by the infringer. In the alternative, the copyright holder may seek statutory damages. These will be determined by the Court, but are usually between #750-$30,000, unless the infringer acted willfully, in which case the damages can go as high as $150,000. If the Court determines that the infringer acted innocently, they may reduce the award to not less than $200. The Court may also award attorney fees and court cost to the copyright holder.

A trademark infringer may be ordered to pay also based on actual damages, as measured by amount of money lost or profit raised by the infringer. An award may be ordered even if there was no actual loss to the trademark holder. The Court can also award the trademark holder the amount of money needed to correct the customer confusion caused by the infringement. If the Court finds the infringer acted intentionally, the award may be multiplied three times.

Third is destruction or impoundment of the infringing articles. For either copyright or trademark infringements, the Court may order all infringing items to be seized and destroyed.

Fourth is criminal penalties. If a copyright infringement is willful, the infringer may be punished criminally up to one year in prison and a fine of up to $10,000. Record and tape piracy penalties are more severe. Trademark infringement is even more severe. Infringing items can be deemed counterfeit goods subjecting the infringer to penalties of up to 5 years in prison and $250,000 fine.

# ACCOUNTING

**E**very new business needs an attorney and an accountant. While many people prepare their own taxes, a good accountant can provide more than just tax preparations. They also provide tax advice, assist with payroll, can help set up your bookkeeping software. If the accountant is familiar with your type of business, they can advise you of the financial standards of your business: what should your labor cost be? How much should you pay for overhead? What is your Cost of Goods Sold? What is your profit margin? These are important numbers for running a successful business.

The first thing every business needs to do is open a bank account. In order to do this, you will need a copy of your Articles of Incorporation or Articles of Organization and your Employer Identification Number. If operating as a sole proprietorship or a single member LLC, you can use your social security number instead of the EIN. Some banks will also require a local occupational license. Investigate the banks to look into costs, convenience, and credibility. If you will be accepting credit cards, you will need to set up a credit card processing system with your bank (It can be a different bank than where you keep your business account). The bank will provide (often lease) you a machine to process the cards. As an alternative, you can use a system such as Square or PayPal.

Next, a business needs to have a bookkeeping system. While old school businesses continue to use a handwritten ledger, the more modern businesses use accounting software. With a good accounting software system, the computer can track all of your expenses and incomes and even sort them based on categories that are business specific. This is important when preparing your tax returns. Most computer accounting programs also can handle your payroll, and some can even print your tax forms (however, for both payroll and taxes, you will need to subscribe to a regular update system). If the idea of bookkeeping is troubling, many accountants offer bookkeeping services too.

Business owners need to start saving receipts. In the event of an audit, the receipts may be necessary to prove the legitimacy of expenses. It is beneficial to get a twelve-month divided folder to put the business receipts in.

The next phase is to set up payroll. Will you be hiring employees or independent contractors; paying weekly or bi-weekly; hourly or commission? If you choose not to use accounting software, it is recommended you hire a payroll service. All businesses are now required to file their payroll tax returns through the Electronic Federal Tax Payment System, requiring internet access.

The business should also register with the Social Security Administration Business Service Online. This is an internet-based service allowing businesses to communicate with the SSA as well as file their W-2 and W-4 forms.

Speaking of W-4, make sure each new employee completes the W-4 so that you can make the correct adjustments for dependents. With each paycheck, the employer is required to holdback a certain percentage of each check for federal income tax, social security tax and Medicaid. In addition, the employer must pay a matching amount. These percentages change on a regular basis, so the proper tax table must be downloaded routinely. All payroll tax records must be saved for at least four years.

Employers must file a quarterly employment tax return (Form 941), an annual unemployment tax return (Form 940), and a W-2 and W-3 in January of each year.

# CORPORATE MAINTENANCE

**A**fter a company has been formed, it has to be maintained. The maintenance obligations are slightly different between corporations and limited liability companies, but the recommendations are not.

Every year corporations are required by law to have a meeting of the shareholders. They can have more than that, but one is required. At this meeting, the shareholders elect the directors of the company for the coming year. Generally, the Board of Directors will give a series of reports, including financial status reports at this meeting. The meeting does not need to be held in Florida- it may be held wherever the Directors deem appropriate, subject to the terms of their by-laws. Many companies try to find attractive locations for their meetings to encourage attendance. So a meeting in Las Vegas or New York is entirely appropriate. Generally, the corporation must send notices of the meeting to all shareholders of record sufficiently in advance to allow them to attend. If the company fails to hold the annual meeting, it does not invalidate the company or its actions, but there may be other consequences I will discuss shortly.

For Limited Liability Companies, there is no such requirement for an annual meeting. However, it is still recommended. It is treated the same as a corporate meeting, with a notice sent out and location to be determined by the Operating Agreement, or in the absence of that designation, at a location selected by the Managers. At an LLC meeting, the Members elect the Managers for the next term.

Of course, both entities must file their annual reports with the Department of State, disclosing their officers, directors and managers. These reports are due between January 1 and May 1 of each year. Failure to file an annual report will subject the company to late fees (currently $400) and eventual administrative dissolution. So, it is usually beneficial for small companies to hold their meetings during this time so they can submit up-to-date information with their annual reports.

Why are these meetings important? If you are going to take the step of forming an entity, it makes sense to maintain it. You wouldn't buy a car and not change the oil. A corporation or LLC needs maintenance just like your car. Things change and the company needs to be able to adapt to those changes. But the other more compelling reason to hold the meetings is to protect the shareholders. Business entities need to be treated like business entities. They are not merely alter egos of the owners. You prove this by keeping them separate. Schedule annual meetings, issue notices or waivers, and take minutes. If proper steps are not taken, when liability arises, the court can allow a party suing the company to reach through the company and go after the individual shareholders. This is called "piercing the corporate veil". When companies are not treated appropriately by their shareholders, such as when the shareholders comingle corporate and personal monies, or fail to do standard corporate maintenance, the Court can deem that the corporation is a sham and allow for personal liability among the shareholders. This destroys the purpose of why the corporation was created in the first place. The easiest way to prevent this from happening is to do corporate maintenance. If the shareholders hold regularly scheduled meetings, follow their bylaws, keep minutes of their meetings, file their annual reports and most importantly, keep the company adequately capitalized and don't comingle their monies, it is rare that a court will pierce the corporate veil.

LLC's get an added benefit here. Under the new LLC law, beginning in January 2014, the failure of an LLC to observe the formalities of acting like a company cannot be used as the basis for finding personal liability among the members. This is because the majority of LLCs are small businesses that often don't know the legalities of corporate activity. But it allows the members added protection from piercing the corporate veil.

I mentioned the annual report above. In the section where I discussed corporate formation I advised that you must provide an email address to the Department of State. This is so they can provide you with a reminder that your annual report is due. However, don't count on this. The reminder is a courtesy, not a requirement. Even with today's technology, some reminders do not get sent out, but the company's filing obligation does not change. As of this writing, the filing fee for corporations is currently $150 and for LLCs is $138.75. Starting May 2 the $400 late fee is due. In years past, if the company did not receive a reminder, they could file an affidavit and the late fee would be waived. That is no longer the case. If the company still does not file the fee by the third Friday of September, the Department of State will administratively dissolve the company. Normally, once a company has been administratively dissolved, they cannot carry on any activity except those necessary to wind down the company. However, the company can be revived at any time thereafter by filing a reinstatement and paying a reinstatement fee. For corporations, this reinstatement fee is $600, but for LLC's it is only $100. Therefore, for an LLC, it is cheaper to let the State dissolve the company and reinstate than it is to pay the late fee. The State will then reinstate the corporation and the corporation will continue as if there had never been a break in status. During the period of dissolution, the State will reserve the company name for one year to make reinstatement easy. However, after one year the name becomes available for others to use. Once the name has been taken by another entity, the corporation must change their name in order to be reinstated.

Corporations (and LLCs) have a duty to advise the State whenever there is any change of status, such as an address change, a change of officers or managers, or a replacement of the registered agent. These changes can be made when filing the annual report. If they occur after the annual report is filed, the company can file an amended annual report (at an additional fee, currently $61.25 for corporations and $50 for LLCs). If the company wants to change its name or change formulation issues such as number of shares that can be issued, they will need to file Articles of Correction (also referred to as Amended Articles of Incorporation (with a filing fee of $35) or Amended Articles of Organization (with a filing fee of $25).

# SHOULD YOU HIRE AN ATTORNEY?

**M**ust you have an attorney to start a business? No. Should you have one? Definitely, but only one who understands business law. A criminal defense attorney is not likely to know the nuances in corporate law to properly advise you. Whether purchasing an existing business or starting one from scratch, there are legal issues all along the way. Every transaction has unique issues that must be dealt with. It may include the Seller assisting with financing, or one of the parties may be from a foreign country, or there may be some assets held back. The details of the transaction need to be planned out and put in writing. It is not unusual for a sale contract to exceed 20 pages. Franchising contracts can exceed 50 pages. Even start-ups can have financing and licensing issues, outside of all the other issues I have outlined in this book.

Aside from buying a home, the start-up of a business will be one of the most important transactions a person can have. The cost can easily be the largest expenditure a person makes in their life. And if done correctly, the return on investment will support the new business owner and their family for the rest of their lives. With an investment of that value, the small additional cost of hiring an attorney to walk through the legal pitfalls is worth it.

There are several items to take into consideration when deciding on hiring an attorney. First is experience. As mentioned before, many attorneys specialize in an area of law (or "concentrate", as the word "specialize" is a legal term indicating the lawyer is certified in an area of law). For example, when I opened my own law practice in 1995 I concentrated on business law and intellectual property. I still maintain that concentration. While I know the basics of the criminal justice system I will not take a criminal case. Nor will I take a divorce case, even though I know the basics of family law. There are nuances in those areas of law that I do not know, and I would be doing the client a disservice by taking their case. While lawyers who specialize may charge a higher fee, because they know their area of law the overall cost may end up being less than hiring a cheaper lawyer who must learn the law. Also, the liability to the client is higher when they hire a lawyer who is less knowledgeable as issues might get missed that a more seasoned attorney may catch.

When investigating lawyers, ask to see their resumes; discuss their experience; look them up on the Florida Bar's website. The Florida Bar website will show if the lawyer has been disciplined during the last ten years. Ask around town about their reputation. Talk with your local clerk of courts, realtors, other businesses.

Also look for attorneys who are willing to educate you. There are many lawyers and legal services who will file your Articles of Incorporation or Organization and then present you with a blank corporate book with no instructions on how to complete it. This is a disservice to the client and borders on unethical. A good business attorney will explain every document to you in detail and explain why certain things are necessary. The lawyers job is to make sure the client knows what, why, how and when.

Next, ask about their billing system so you know what to expect. Legal fees can be billed in many ways:

Hourly: The primary billing method is hourly. In an hourly billing system, the attorney keeps track of how many minutes he works on a case and bills the client based on how much time he spent. As an example, if the lawyer bills at $300 per hour and spends thirty minutes on a hearing, he will bill $150. The problem with this fee arrangement is that the legal fees may quickly add up.

Flat Fee: In a flat fee system, the attorney charges a fixed amount regardless of how much work he has to do. With the flat fee, the attorney makes the same whether he can do the work in one day or if it takes six months. The downside to this fee system is that it gives the attorney incentive to finish working more quickly, sometimes at the cost of quality.

Contingent Fee: In a contingent fee case, the attorney gets a portion of whatever recovery the client receives. Usually the percentage is around 30% (Florida law set out a sliding scale for contingent fees that runs between 30 and 40%). This doesn't really apply to business start-ups, although some lawyers will take a percentage of the business as payment.

Pro Bono: This is a free case for the client. Every attorney in Florida is required to do a certain amount of pro bono work or pay into a pool for others to provide free legal services. If the attorney determines that you qualify, they may be willing to work at no cost.

# CLOSING

**H**opefully this book has provided you with some information on how to start your own business. If proper planning and research are done, starting your own business can be an exciting and rewardable venture. But it comes with work. Having a reputable attorney and accountant can take care of a lot of the stress that comes with starting a business, but you have to be an active participant. As you move forward you may find you rely less on them as you develop knowledge of business issues.

As mentioned at the outset, the information being provided in this book is not designed to be specific legal advice. It is offered for information purposes only. If anything you have read here has created questions regarding your situation, contact a business attorney in your area.

# APPENDIX 1: SAMPLE ARTICLES OF INCORPORATION

### ARTICLES OF INCORPORATION
### FOR
### (COMPANY NAME), INC.

The undersigned hereby forms a Florida for profit corporation pursuant to Florida Statutes 607 and 621, and hereby adopt the following Articles of Incorporation:

**ARTICLE 1.** Name: The name of the Corporation is
_____ (Company Name), INC..

**ARTICLE 2.**   Address: The initial mailing address of the Corporation is _____.
The physical address of the company shall be _____
_____

**ARTICLE 3.**   Registered Agent, Registered Office, & Registered Agent's Signature:   The name and the Florida street address of the Registered Agent are:

_____ (Name)
_____ (Street)
_____ (City/State/ZIP)

*Having been named as registered agent and to accept service of process for the above stated Corporation at the place designated in this certificate, I hereby accept the appointment as registered agent and agree to act in this capacity. I further agree to comply with the provisions of all statutes relating to the proper and complete performance of my duties, and I am familiar with and accept the obligations of my position as registered agent as provided for in Chapter 608, F.S.*

_____

Signature of registered agent

**ARTICLE 4.** Initial Officers and Directors: The names and addresses of the initial Directors are:

_____ (Name)
_____ (Street)
_____ (City/State/ZIP)

The initial officers of the corporation shall be as follows:

President: _____

Vice President:_____

Secretary: _____

Treasurer: _____

**ARTICLE 5.** Shares: The corporation shall be authorized to issue _____ (total number of shares) shares of stock with $_____ par value.

**ARTICLE 6.** Purpose: The Company shall have all powers that may be held by Florida For Profit companies under the laws of the State of Florida as they may be amended from time to time. The purpose for which the Company is organized is the transaction of any or all lawful business for which corporations may be organized under the laws of the State of Florida as they may be amended from time to time.

**ARTICLE 7.** Incorporator: The name and address of the Incorporator is

_____ (Name)
_____ (Street)
_____ (City/State/ZIP)

IN WITNESS WHEREOF, we the undersigned incorporators have set our hands on the date indicated below.

Date:_____
Signature: _____
          Incorporator

# APPENDIX 2: SAMPLE ARTICLES OF ORGANIZATION

## ARTICLES OF ORGANIZATION
### FOR
_____ (COMPANY NAME), LLC

A FLORIDA LIMITED LIABILITY COMPANY

The undersigned hereby form a limited liability company ("LLC") under the Florida Limited Liability Company Act and hereby adopt the following Articles of Organization of the LLC:

**ARTICLE 1.** Name: The name of the Limited Liability Company is _____ (Company name), LLC.

**ARTICLE 2.** Address: The initial mailing address of the Limited Liability Company is _____ _____.

The physical address of the company shall be _____ _____

**ARTICLE 3.**   Registered Agent, Registered Office, & Registered Agent's Signature:    The name and the Florida street address of the Registered Agent are:

_____ (Name)
_____ (Street)
_____ (City/State/ZIP)

*Having been named as registered agent and to accept service of process for the above stated limited liability company at the place designated in this certificate, I hereby accept the appointment as registered agent and agree to act in this capacity.    I further agree to comply with the provisions of all statutes relating to the proper and complete performance of my duties, and I am familiar with and accept the obligations of my position as registered agent as provided for in Chapter 605, F.S.*

_____
Signature of registered agent

**ARTICLE 4.** Management:    The Limited Liability Company is to be [member managed/manager managed]    The initial managers shall be   _____

**ARTICLE 5.**   Powers:    The Company shall have all powers that may be held by limited liability companies under the laws of the State of Florida as they may be amended from time to time. The purpose for which the Company is organized is the transaction of any or all lawful business for which limited liability companies may be organized under the laws of the State of Florida as they may be amended from time to time.

**ARTICLE 6.**   Operating Agreement: The members shall enter into an Operating Agreement which relates to the business of the Company, the conduct of its affairs, its rights or powers and the rights or powers of its members, managers, officers, employees or agents.

IN WITNESS WHEREOF, we the undersigned organizers have set our hands on the date indicated below.


Date:_____

Signature: _____

# APPENDIX 3: BYLAWS

CORPORATE BY-LAWS FOR

_____

ARTICLE I: CORPORATE OFFICE: The Corporation's principal office shall be located at _____
_____, in the city of
_____, in the state of
_____. Various offices may exist for the corporation, either within or outside _____, as the board of directors may designate or as the business of the corporation may require.

ARTICLE II: MEETINGS OF THE SHAREHOLDERS

1) MEETINGS: Pursuant to Florida Statutes 607.0701, the corporation shall hold an annual meeting on the anniversary of the filing of the articles of incorporation or on any other day selected by the Directors. At the meeting, the shareholders shall elect directors and transact such business as may be deemed necessary. Meetings of the shareholders shall be at the principal place of business of the corporation or at a place designated by the board of directors.

2) SPECIAL MEETINGS: A special meeting may be called by the president, board of directors or a written request by

the shareholders. A meeting requested by the shareholders shall be called for, at a date not less than 14 or more than 60 days after the request is made.

3) NOTICE OF MEETING: The president, secretary, officer or director of the corporation may give notice of a meeting. This notice must be in written form and must state the place, day and hour of the meeting and in the case of a special meeting must state the purpose for which the meeting is called. The notice must be addressed to the shareholder at his address as it appears on the stock transfer books of the corporation. When a meeting is adjourned to another time, it will not be necessary to give any notice of the adjourned meeting provided that the time and place to which the meeting is adjourned is announced at the meeting at which the adjournment is taken.

4) QUORUM: A quorum at a meeting of shareholders shall be 50%+1 of the shares entitled to vote, represented in person or by proxy. The affirmative vote of a majority of the shares represented at the meeting and entitled to vote shall constitute a binding act unless otherwise provided by law.

5) PROXY: Every shareholder, entitled to vote at a meeting of shareholders, may authorize another person or persons to act for him by proxy. All proxies must be executed in writing by the shareholder or his duly authorized and must be filed with the secretary of the corporation before or at the time of the meeting. Each proxy shall be valid only for the meeting specified in the proxy.

6) VOTING OF SHARES: Each outstanding share entitled to vote at a meeting, shall have the right to one vote, in person or by proxy, upon each matter submitted to a vote at such meeting.

7) ACTION TAKEN BY SHAREHOLDERS WITHOUT A MEETING: Any action, within the laws of the corporation, may be taken without prior notice of a meeting or without a vote, provided that a written consent setting forth the action so taken is signed by the shareholders who are entitled to vote in the corporation and whose votes would be necessary to authorize or take such action at a said meeting.

ARTICLE III: BOARD OF DIRECTORS

1) POWERS: The board of directors shall manage the business of the corporation and exercise its corporate powers as allowed under Florida Statutes.

2) NUMBER OF DIRECTORS AND THEIR TERMS: There shall be a minimum number of _____ director(s) for the corporation. Each director shall be elected at the annual shareholder's meeting and shall hold office until the next annual meeting of shareholders and until his successor is elected and qualified.

3) VACANCIES: A qualified person may be appointed to fill a vacancy on the board of directors by an affirmative vote of the majority of the remaining directors. The incoming director shall hold office for the rest of the term and until his successor is elected and qualified.

4) RESIGNATIONS: A Director may resign at any time during their term. Written notice must be filed with the secretary or president of the corporation; and unless otherwise specified in the notice, said resignation shall take effect upon receipt thereof and acceptance of the resignation shall not be necessary to make it effective.

5) REMOVAL OF DIRECTORS: Any and all of the directors may be removed with or without cause by a vote of the majority of holders of stock who are authorized to vote at an election of directors.

6) NOTICES: A written notice for any and all meetings must be given no earlier than 14 days or more than 60 days. This notice must be in written form and must state the place, day and hour of the meeting and in the case of a special meeting must state the purpose for which the meeting is called. The notice must be addressed to the director at his address as it appears on the records of the corporation.

7) ANNUAL MEETINGS: The board of directors shall designate the place, time and date of their meeting. Notices of said meeting must be sent to all directors unless stated at the previous meetings where all directors are present.

8) SPECIAL MEETINGS: Special meetings of the board shall be held upon notice to the directors and may be called by the president upon at least a 5 day notice to each director personally or by email. Notice of a meeting need not be given to any director who submits a waiver of notice whether before or after the meeting.

9) QUORUM: A majority of the directors shall constitute a quorum for the transaction of business. If at any meeting of the board there shall be less than a quorum present, a majority of those present may adjourn the meeting.

10) ACTION TAKEN WITHOUT A MEETING: Any action that may be taken by the board of directors at a meeting may be taken without a meeting if a consent in writing, setting forth the action so to be taken, shall be signed before

such action by all the directors.

## ARTICLE IV: CORPORATE OFFICERS

1) OFFICES AND ELECTIONS: The board of directors may elect a president, vice-president, secretary, treasurer and any other officers or assistant officers as deemed necessary. Officers shall perform tasks as normally performed by those positions or those tasks set out by the directors.  These officers shall serve a term of one year and will hold office until their successor is elected and qualified. The officers for the corporation shall be appointed at the annual meeting of the board. Any two or more offices may be held by the same person.

2) VACANCIES: In the event of death, resignation or removal of an officer from office, the board of directors shall appoint a successor to fill the open term. Any officer elected or appointed by the board may be removed by the board with or without cause.

## ARTICLE V: STOCK CERTIFICATES

1) ISSUANCE: Certificates of shares shall be issued to every shareholder. Certificates must be paid in full before issuance can take place. Corporate certificates of shares must be signed by the president and secretary and must be sealed with the corporate seal.

2) TRANSFER OF SHARES: Transfer of shares of the corporation shall be made only on the stock transfer book of the corporation, by the Secretary of the corporation or the corporate legal counsel. The person in whose name shares stand on the corporate transfer ledger shall be

deemed to be the owner thereof for all purposes.

3) LOST, STOLEN OR DESTROYED CERTIFICATES: If certificates of shares are claimed to be lost, stolen or destroyed, a new certificate shall be issued upon receipt of proper affidavit. The affidavit must reflect ownership of the person claiming the certificate and state how the certificate was lost. Upon deposit of a bond or other indemnity in such amount decided by the board of directors and at their discretion, the certificate of stock shall be replaced.

ARTICLE VI: CORPORATE RECORDS AND BOOKS

1) RESPONSIBILITIES: The Corporation shall maintain accurate books, records and minutes of all the board of directors, shareholders and officers' meetings, as well as all records required to be kept by Florida Statutes. The corporation book shall be maintained at the principal office or such other place as designated by the Directors.

2) SHAREHOLDER'S INSPECTION RIGHTS: Shareholders shall be allowed to examine, at a reasonable time, in person or by agent or by an attorney, the corporate books and records of accounts, minutes and records of shareholders. Copies of such records can only be made upon written request disclosing good cause.

3) FINANCIAL RECORDS: Four months after the close of each corporate fiscal year, the corporation shall prepare a balance sheet and a profit and loss statement showing in reasonable detail the financial condition of the corporation. Upon written request, the corporation shall issue to any shareholder or holder of voting trust certificates of shares in the corporation, a copy of the most recent balance sheet

and profit and loss statement, showing in reasonable detail the financial condition of the corporation. These records shall be filed in the corporate office and shall be kept on file for a minimum of ____ years and may be subject to inspection during business hours by any shareholder or holder of voting trust certificates, in person or by an appointed agent.

4) DIVIDENDS: Dividends may be declared by the board of directors on its shares in property, cash or its own shares, except when the corporation is insolvent or when payment of said dividends would render the corporation insolvent.

ARTICLE VII: FISCAL YEAR: The Corporation's fiscal year shall begin with the first day of January in each year.

ARTICLE VIII: AMENDMENTS: These by-laws may be altered, amended or repealed and new by-laws may be adopted by the board of directors at any regular or special meeting of the board of directors.
Date:

Secretary: _____

# APPENDIX 4: SHAREHOLDER'S AGREEMENT

SHAREHOLDERS AGREEMENT

THIS SHAREHOLDERS AGREEMENT is made by and among
_____ ("Shareholder 1"),
_____ ("Shareholder 2"), and
_____ ("Shareholder 3") (Shareholder 1,
Shareholder 2 and Shareholder 3 and any subsequent person or
entity holding common stock of the Company hereinafter
sometimes referred to individually as a "Shareholder" and
collectively as the "Shareholders") and
_____, a Florida corporation (the
"Company").

WITNESSETH: WHEREAS, in order to insure the harmonious
and successful management and control of the Company, and to
provide for an orderly and fair disposition of shares of common
stock of the Company now or hereafter owned by any
Shareholder;

NOW, THEREFORE, in consideration of the mutual promises of
the parties hereto, and intending to be legally bound, the parties
hereby agree as follows:

1. Definitions.
(a) "Offering Shareholder" means any Shareholder, or his
personal representatives, heirs, administrators, and executors, as

the case may be, who pursuant to this Agreement must or does offer all or any of his Shares to the Company or the Continuing Shareholders.

(b) "Continuing Shareholders" means all Shareholders other than an Offering Shareholder.

(c) "Shares" means shares of Common Stock of the Company now or hereafter owned by any Shareholder.

(d) "Buyer" means the Company or those Continuing Shareholders who purchase an Offering Shareholder's Shares pursuant to this Agreement.

(e) "Management Shareholder" means Shareholder 1, Shareholder 2 and Shareholder 3.

(f) "Nonmanagement Shareholder" means any Shareholder other than a Management Shareholder.

2. Purchase for Investment. Each Shareholder represents and warrants that he is acquiring and has acquired his Shares for his own account for investment and not with a view to, or for resale in connection with, any distribution thereof or with any present intent of selling any portion thereof.

3. Transfers of Shares. Except for security for the purchase of shares in the Company, a Shareholder may not transfer, give, convey, sell, pledge, bequeath, donate, assign, encumber or otherwise dispose of any Shares except pursuant to this Agreement. Shares may not be sold to any third party without the unanimous consent to all Continuing Shareholders.

(a) Transfers to the Company. Notwithstanding anything to the contrary contained in this Agreement, a Shareholder may give, sell, transfer or otherwise dispose of all or any of his Shares to the Company at such price and on such terms and conditions as such Shareholder and the Board of Directors of the Company may agree.

(b) Transfer to Others. Except as provided for in Paragraph 3(a) above, a Shareholder desiring to dispose of some or all of his

Shares may do so only pursuant to a bona fide offer to purchase (the "Offer") and after compliance with the following provisions. Such Shareholder shall first give written notice to the Company and the other Shareholders of his intention to dispose of his Shares, identifying the number of Shares he desires to dispose of, the proposed purchase price per Share and the name of the proposed purchaser and attaching an exact copy of the Offer received by such Shareholder.

(i) The Company's Right to Purchase. The Company shall have the exclusive right to purchase all of the Shares which the Offering Shareholder proposes to sell at the proposed purchase price per Share. The Company shall exercise this right to purchase by giving written notice to the Offering Shareholder (with a copy thereof to each of the Continuing Shareholders) within thirty (30) days after receipt of the notice from the Offering Shareholder (the "30 Day Period") that the Company elects to purchase the Shares subject to the Offer and setting forth a date and time for closing which shall be not later than forty-five (45) days after the date of such notice from the Company. At the time of closing, the Offering Shareholder shall deliver to the Company certificates representing the Shares to be sold, together with stock powers duly endorsed in blank. The Shares shall be delivered by the Offering Shareholder free of any and all liens and encumbrances. All transfer taxes and documentary stamps shall be paid by the Offering Shareholder.

(ii) The Continuing Shareholders Right to Purchase. If the Company fails to exercise its right to purchase pursuant to subparagraph (i) above, the Continuing Shareholders individually shall have the right for an additional period of thirty (30) days (the "Additional 30 Day Period") commencing at the expiration of the 30 Day Period to purchase the Shares which the Offering Shareholder proposes to sell at the proposed purchase price per Share. Any Continuing Shareholders desiring to exercise this right to purchase shall give written notice to the Offering Shareholder prior to the expiration of the Additional 30 Day

Period that they elect to purchase his Shares and setting forth a date and time for closing which shall be not later than forty-five (45) days after the expiration of the Additional 30 Day Period. Any purchase of Shares by all or some of the Continuing Shareholders shall be made in such proportion as they might agree among themselves or, in the absence of any such agreement, pro rata in proportion to their ownership of Shares of the Company (excluding the Offering Shareholder's Shares) at the time of such offer, but in any event one or more of the Continuing Shareholders must agree to purchase all the Shares which the Offering Shareholder proposes to sell. At the time of closing, the Offering Shareholder shall deliver to Buyer certificates representing the Shares to be sold, together with stock powers duly endorsed in blank. Said Shares shall be delivered by the offering Shareholder free and clear of any and all liens and encumbrances. All transfer taxes and documentary stamps shall be paid by the Offering Shareholder.

(iii) Performance of Acceptance. When exercising the rights granted in Paragraphs 3(b)(i) and (ii) hereof, Buyer must elect to purchase all Shares which the Offering Shareholder proposes to sell for the price and upon the same terms for payment of the price as are set forth in the Offer; provided, however, that if said offer received by the Offering Shareholder shall provide for any act or action to be done or performed by the party making such Offer at any time before or within thirty (30) days after the last day for exercise of Buyer's right to purchase pursuant to Paragraphs 3(b)(i) and (ii) hereof, then the Buyer shall be deemed to have complied with the terms and conditions of such Offer if Buyer does or performs such act or action within thirty (30) days after the last day for exercise of Buyer's right to purchase pursuant to Paragraphs 3(b)(i) and(ii) hereof.

(iv) Sale to Third Party. If either the Company or some or all of the Continuing Shareholders do not elect to purchase all of the Shares which the Offering Shareholder proposes to sell, the Offering Shareholder may accept the Offer which the Offering

Shareholder mailed with his notice to the Company pursuant to Paragraph 3(b) hereof and transfer all (but not less than all) of the Shares which he proposes to sell pursuant thereto on the same terms and conditions set forth in such Offer, provided that any transferee of such Shares shall be bound by this Agreement, and further provided that if such sale is not completed within one hundred twenty (120) days after the date notice is received by the Company under Paragraph 3(b) hereof, all such Shares shall again become subject to the restrictions and provisions of this Agreement.

(v) Right of Co-Sale. Notwithstanding any other provision hereof, in the event the Offering Shareholder receives an Offer from an unaffiliated third party (the "Offeror") to purchase from such Shareholder not less than 20% of the Shares owned by such Shareholder and such Shareholder intends to accept such Offer, the Offering Shareholder shall, after complying with the provisions of Paragraph 3(b)(i) and (ii) above and before accepting such Offer, forward a copy of such Offer to the Company and each of the Continuing Shareholders. The Offering Shareholder shall not sell any such Shares to the Offeror unless the terms of the Offer are extended by the Offeror to the Continuing Shareholders pro rata in proportion to their ownership of Shares of the Company (excluding the Offering Shareholder's Shares) at the time of such Offer. The Continuing Shareholders shall have 10 days from the date of the foregoing Offer to accept such Offer.

4. Right of First Refusal.
(a) Except in the case of Excluded Securities (as defined below), the Company shall not issue, sell or exchange, agree to issue, sell or exchange, or reserve or set aside for issuance, sale or exchange, any (i) shares of Common Stock or any other equity security of the Company which is convertible into Common Stock or any other equity security of the Company, (ii) any debt security of the Company which is convertible into Common Stock or any other

equity security of the Company, or (iii) any option, warrant or other right to subscribe for, purchase or otherwise acquire any equity security or any such debt security of the Company, unless in each case the Company shall have first offered to sell to each Shareholder, pro rata in proportion to such Shareholder's then ownership of Shares of the Company, such securities (the "Offered Securities") (and to sell thereto such Offered Securities not subscribed for by the other Shareholders as hereinafter provided), at a price and on such other terms as shall have been specified by the Company in writing delivered to such Shareholder (the "Stock Offer"), which Stock Offer by its terms shall remain open and irrevocable for a period of 10 days (subject to extension pursuant to the last sentence of subsection (b) below) from the date it is delivered by the Company to the Shareholder.

(b) Notice of each Shareholder's intention to accept, in whole or in part, a Stock Offer shall be evidenced by a writing signed by such Shareholder and delivered to the Company prior to the end of the 10-day period of such Stock Offer, setting forth such portion of the Offered Securities as such Shareholder elects to purchase (the "Notice of Acceptance"). If any Shareholder shall subscribe for less than his pro rata share of the Offered Securities to be sold, the other subscribing Shareholders shall be entitled to purchase the balance of that Shareholder's pro rata share in the same proportion in which they were entitled to purchase the Offered Securities in the first instance (excluding for such purposes such Shareholder), provided any such other Shareholder elected by a Notice of Acceptance to purchase all of his pro rata share of the Offered Securities. The Company shall notify each Shareholder within 5 days following the expiration of the 10-day period described above of the amount of Offered Securities which each Shareholder may purchase pursuant to the foregoing sentence, and each Shareholder shall then have l0 days from the delivery of such notice to indicate such additional amount, if any, that such Shareholder wishes to purchase.

(c) In the event that Notices of Acceptance are not given by the

Shareholders in respect of all the Offered Securities, the Company shall have 120 days from the expiration of the foregoing 10-day or 25-day period, whichever is applicable, to sell all or any part of such Offered Securities as to which a Notice of Acceptance has not been given by the Shareholders (the "Refused Securities") to any other person or persons, but only upon terms and conditions in all respects, including, without limitation, unit price and interest rates, which are no more favorable, in the aggregate, to such other person or persons or less favorable to the Company than those set forth in the Stock Offer. Upon the closing, which shall include full payment to the Company, of the sale to such other person or persons of all the Refused Securities, the Shareholders shall purchase from the Company, and the Company shall sell to the Shareholders the Offered Securities in respect of which Notices of Acceptance were delivered to the Company by the Shareholders, at the terms specified in the Stock Offer.

(d) In each case, any Offered Securities not purchased by the Shareholders or other person or persons in accordance with Section 4(c) may not be sold or otherwise disposed of until they are again offered to the Shareholders under the procedures specified in Sections 4(a), (b) and (c).

(e) The rights of the Shareholders under this Section 4 shall not apply to the following securities (the "Excluded Securities"): (i) Any (A) shares of Common Stock or any other equity security of the Company which is convertible into Common Stock or any other equity security of the Company, (B) debt security of the Company which is convertible into Common Stock or any other equity security of the Company, or (C) option, warrant or other right to subscribe for, purchase or otherwise acquire any equity security or any such debt security of the Company (collectively, an "Equity Security") if the issuance of such Equity Security does not alter the respective proportions of ownership (on a fully diluted basis) by Shareholder 1, Shareholder 2 and Shareholder 3, as among themselves, of Equity Securities immediately prior to the issuance of such Equity Security; (ii) Common Stock issued as a stock dividend or upon any stock split or other subdivision or combination of the outstanding shares of Common Stock; (iii) Securities issued pursuant to the acquisition by the Company of another corporation to the stockholders of such other corporation by merger or purchase of substantially all of the assets whereby the Company owns not less than 51% of the voting power of such other corporation; and (iv) Common Stock issued in connection with a firm underwritten public offering of shares of Common Stock, registered pursuant to the Securities Act.

5. Sale Or Redemption Upon Termination of Employment or Upon Disability Or Upon Death. Upon the termination of a Shareholder's employment or other relationship with the Company (including without limitation, any position as an officer, director, consultant, joint venturer, independent contractor, or promoter to or of the Company) for whatever reason, the Disability (as defined below) of a Shareholder, or the death of a Shareholder (any such event hereinafter a "Triggering Event"), such Shareholder (the "Terminated Shareholder")(or his heirs, executors, guardian or personal representative) within sixty (60) days after the Triggering Event shall sell all, but not less than all, of the Shares owned by the Shareholder to the Company, which Company shall then redistribute those shares on a pro rata basis to the remaining Shareholders. For purposes of this Agreement, "Disability" of a particular person means the inability, due to a physical or mental condition, of such person to maintain his employment or other relationship with the Company (including without limitation, fulfilling his duties in any position as an officer, director, consultant, joint venturer, independent contractor, or promoter to or of the Company) or to conduct his normal daily activities on behalf of the Corporation for any six (6) consecutive month period. Despite the foregoing, as the founding Shareholder, Bert L. Shareholder 1 shall retain all shares owned by him regardless of his employment status or ability to

work. Upon death, all dividends payable to the deceased Shareholder shall cease and shall be retained by the company.

6. Purchase Price. The purchase price for all Shares purchased pursuant to Paragraph 5 hereof shall be $_____ per share.

7. Payment of Purchase Price. The purchase price for all Shares purchased pursuant to Paragraph 5 hereof shall be paid over a period of _____ (____) years at _____ percent (_____%) interest.

8. Put and Call Options
(a) Put and Call Options. Each Shareholder shall have the right and option upon the written declaration (a "Declaration") by such Shareholder to the other Shareholders and the Company of the occurrence of an "impasse" (as defined below) to sell to the Continuing Shareholders all of his Shares, and the Continuing Shareholders shall have the obligation to either (i) purchase all of such Shares owned by the offering Shareholder in such proportion as the Continuing Shareholders may agree upon, and if they cannot so agree, pro rata in proportion to their then ownership of Shares of the Company (excluding the Offering Shareholder's Shares) or (ii) if the Continuing Shareholders are unable or unwilling to purchase all of the Shares owned by the Offering Shareholder, sell all of their Shares to the Offering Shareholder, and the Offering Shareholder shall have the obligation to buy such Shares.
(b) Impasse. An "impasse" shall be conclusively evidenced by (i) either Shareholder 1, Shareholder 3 or Shareholder 2 or their respective representative, voting opposite the others at a vote at a shareholders meeting or at a vote at a meeting of the Board of Directors of the Company (or failing to attend such meetings upon due notice if such failure results in the lack of a quorum making such vote impossible), which vote is on a material issue,

not in the ordinary course of business, and affecting the business, assets or operations of the Company, including, but not limited to, a proposal to merge, liquidate, consolidate or dissolve the Company, or to sell, lease or dispose of all or substantially all of the assets of the Company or to amend the substantive provisions of the Company's bylaws or articles of incorporation, or to issue or redeem stock, or to declare dividends of any kind, and (ii) either Shareholder 1, Shareholder 3 or Shareholder 2 notifying the others and the Company and any other Shareholders within thirty (30) days after such meeting, proposed meeting or vote than an "impasse" has occurred. The put and call rights granted to each Shareholder under this Paragraph 8 are independent of the other rights granted to the Shareholders and the Company under the other terms of this Agreement and such rights are not mutually exclusive or inconsistent.

(c) Exercise of Option. The Continuing Shareholders shall exercise any option provided for in this Paragraph 8 within thirty (30) days after receipt of a declaration. Any closing of the sale of Shares pursuant to such exercise shall occur within ninety (90) days after receipt of a Declaration.

(d) Purchase Price. Any purchase or sale of Shares sold pursuant to this Paragraph 8 shall be at the price as set forth in the Declaration delivered by the Shareholder exercising his right to sell his shares and shall be paid at the closing of the sale of the Shares.

9. Agreement Binding on All Persons Interested in Shares. Each person who now or hereafter acquires any legal or equitable interest in any Shares shall be bound by the terms of this Agreement. No issuance or transfer of Shares shall be effective and the Company shall not enter any issue or transfer upon the stock books of the Company or issue a certificate in the name of any person unless the Company is satisfied that such person is, and in a manner satisfactory to the Company has acknowledged being, bound by this Agreement.

10. Closing. Except as otherwise agreed to or expressly provided for herein, closing pursuant to the exercise of a right to purchase or sell Shares pursuant to this Agreement shall be held at the principal executive offices of the Company.

11. Entry of Legend Upon Stock Certificates. The following legend shall be immediately entered on each stock certificate representing Shares owned by the Shareholders: "The gift, sale, mortgage, pledge, hypothecation or other encumbering or transfer of the shares of the capital stock represented by this certificate is restricted in accordance with the terms and conditions of a Shareholders Agreement dated the _____ day of _____, _____, a copy of which is on file at the principal executive offices of the Company. Said Shareholders Agreement restricts the ability of the Shareholder to sell, give, pledge, bequeath or otherwise transfer or dispose of this stock certificate and the shares of capital stock represented by it."

12. After Acquired Shares -- Subsequent Shareholders. The terms and conditions of this Agreement shall specifically apply not only to Shares owned by Shareholders at the time of execution of this Agreement, but also to any Shares acquired by any Shareholder subsequent to such execution.

13. Board of Directors. At the Annual Meeting of the Shareholders, the Shareholders shall elect the members of the Board of Directors. At each election of the Board of Directors of the Company, the Shareholders shall vote their Shares to elect _____ directors of the Company.

14. Community and Marital Property Laws. The parties agree and acknowledge that their spouse does not and cannot have any interest in and to the shares of the company. Notwithstanding anything to the contrary contained herein, the following terms

shall control to the extent community property laws or other marital property laws apply to the Shares of any Shareholder:

(a) Lifetime Transfers. The provisions of this Agreement regarding restrictions against the transfer of Shares shall apply to any interest of the spouse of any Shareholder in such Shares (said spouse is hereinafter referred to as a "Spouse").

(b) Marital Dissolution. Any decree of dissolution, separate maintenance agreement or other property settlement between a Shareholder and his or her Spouse shall provide that the entire marital property interest of the Spouse in the Shares of the Shareholder shall be granted to the Shareholder as part of the division of the property of the marriage and the Spouse shall release and the Shareholder shall accept any marital property interest of such Spouse in the Shares. If payment for such Shares is ordered by the Court or demanded by the Spouse, no consideration shall be required, but if the Shareholder volunteers consideration for said release of interest it shall be no greater than $_____ per share.

(d) Inclusion of Marital Property. Any purchase of the Shares of a Shareholder pursuant to any provision of this Agreement shall include without limitation or condition the entire marital property interest of the Spouse of such Shareholder in the Shares being purchased.

15. Insurance. The Company may, if it so desires, purchase insurance policies on the life of any Management Shareholder as key man insurance. If any Shareholder on whose life the Company owns an insurance policy shall at any time during his lifetime sell all of his Shares, then that Shareholder shall have the right to purchase from the Company the insurance policy or policies on his life at the cash surrender value, if any. The Company shall deliver the policy or policies on the life of such Shareholder upon payment of the cash surrender value, if any, end shall execute any necessary instruments of transfer and change of beneficiary forms. In addition to the foregoing, the Company

shall purchase term life insurance on the life of each Shareholder in an amount sufficient to repurchase such Shareholder's stock in the Company from the Shareholder's heirs.

16. Subchapter S Election. All the Shareholders agree that it is in the Corporation's best interest to elect to be treated as a Subchapter S Corporation, within the meaning of Section 1361 of the Internal Revenue Code of 1986.   In order to maintain such S status, notwithstanding anything provided in this Agreement herein to the contrary, no Shareholder or successor may transfer, and no person may acquire, the beneficial ownership of any Share if such transfer or acquisition would cause the Corporation's S status to terminate, including but not limited to, transfers to, or acquisitions by:    (a) any person who would cause the Corporation to have more than 35 shareholders; (b) any nonresident alien; or (c) any person other than an individual or an estate.   The Corporation's board of directors, may, in their sole and absolute discretion, impose such other restrictions upon the sale or transfer of Shares as they shall deem appropriate to maintain the Corporation's S status.

17. Pro Rata Allocations. All items of income and loss of the Company shall be assigned pro rata to each day throughout the year. However, the Shareholders hereby consent to make an election pursuant to Section 1362(c)(3) of the Code or Section 1377(a)(2) of the Code in the event that the Board of Directors determines such elections to be in the best interest of a majority of the Shareholders.

18. Authorization. The Company is authorized to enter into this Agreement by virtue of a resolution passed at a meeting of the Board of Directors.

19. Notices. Notices and declarations under this Agreement shall be in writing and sent by registered or certified mail, return

receipt requested, postage paid, to the Company at its principal executive offices and to Shareholders at their last address as shown on the records of the Company or at such other address with respect to any party hereto as such party shall notify the other Shareholders and the Company in writing in the manner specified herein.

20. Deposits of Certificates. The parties to this agreement agreed to deposit their certificates for the stock with the secretary of the corporation for retention in the corporate book as long as the certificates are subject to this agreement. During the term of such deposit, the respective parties shall be entitled to all rights in the respective shares other than physical possession of the certificates.

21. Severability. The various provisions of this Agreement are severable from each other and from the other provisions of the Agreement, and in the event that any provision in this Agreement shall be held to be invalid or unenforceable by a court of competent jurisdiction, the remainder of this Agreement shall be fully effective, operative and enforceable.

22. Free end Clear of Encumbrances. All Shares sold pursuant to the terms of this Agreement shall be free of any and all liens and encumbrances and accompanied by stock powers duly endorsed in blank.

23. Binding Effect. This Agreement shall be binding upon and inure to the benefit of the parties hereto and their respective heirs, personal representatives, executors, administrators, successors and assigns.

24. Gender. Pronouns used herein are to be interpreted as referring to both the masculine and feminine gender.

25. Governing Law. This Agreement shall be construed and interpreted in accordance with the laws of the State of Florida. Any litigation brought under or in regards to this agreement shall be filed only in _____, _____ County, Florida.

26. Specific Performance. The parties hereto declare that it is impossible to measure in money the damages which accrue to a party hereto or to his estate, by reason of a failure to perform any of the obligations of this Agreement. Therefore, if any party hereto or the personal representative of a decedent shall institute any action or proceeding to enforce the provisions hereof, any other party against whom such action or proceeding is brought shall have no right to make the claim or defense therein, that such party or such personal representative has an adequate remedy at law. The parties further agree that the shares of Stock are unique chattels and that the equitable remedy of specific performance shall be available to enforce the terms of this Agreement.

27. Termination. This agreement shall terminate on any one of the following events:

(A) the written agreement of all the parties to the agreement;

(B) the dissolution, bankruptcy, or insolvency of the company;

(C) at such time as only one shareholder remains, the shares of the others having been transferred or redeemed.

28. Entire Agreement. This instrument contains the entire agreement of the parties and may be changed only by an agreement in writing signed by the Company and all persons then owning Shares.

29. Counterparts. This Agreement may be executed in one or more counterparts each of which shall be deemed an original and

all of which together shall be deemed to be one and the same instrument.

IN WITNESS WHEREOF, the parties hereto have duly executed this Agreement on the day and year set forth below.

_____ Shareholder 1
_____ Date

_____ Shareholder 2
_____ Date

_____ Shareholder 3
_____ Date

# APPENDIX 5: SAMPLE OPERATING AGREEMENT

OPERATING AGREEMENT
of
[COMPANY NAME], LLC
This Limited Liability Company Operating Agreement (the "Agreement") is made and entered into as of
_____  _____, 2018, by and among [Manager Name], whose address is [Manager Address], as Members and Managers (sometimes hereinafter referred to as "Manager") of [COMPANY NAME], LLC (the "Company"), and such parties who from time to time execute this Agreement as Members. The parties hereto desire to form the Company pursuant to the provisions of Chapter 605, Florida Statutes (the "Statute") to engage in the business hereinafter described upon the terms and conditions hereinafter set forth.

The purpose of this Operating Agreement is among other things to govern the relations among the members as members and between the members and the limited liability company, the rights and duties under Chapter 605 of a person in the capacity of manager, the activities and affairs of the company and the conduct of those activities and affairs, and the means and conditions for amending the operating agreement.

Despite anything within to the contrary, this operating agreement shall not:

(a)  Vary the limited liability company's capacity under Florida Statutes 605.0109 to sue and be sued in its own name.

(b)  Vary the governing law applicable under Florida Statutes 605.0104.

(c)  Vary the requirement, procedure, or other provision of Chapter 605 pertaining to:

1.  Registered agents; or

2.  The department, including provisions pertaining to records authorized or required to be delivered to the department for filing under Chapter 605.

(d)  Vary the signing and filing of records under judicial order provisions of Florida Statutes 605.0204.

(e)  Eliminate the duty of loyalty or the duty of care under Florida Statutes 605.04091, except as otherwise provided in subsection (4).

(f)  Eliminate the obligation of good faith and fair dealing under Florida Statutes 605.04091.

(g)  Relieve or exonerate a person from liability for conduct involving bad faith, willful or intentional misconduct, or a knowing violation of law.

(h)  Unreasonably restrict the duties and rights stated in Florida Statutes 605.0410 regarding record keeping, access and inspection rights.

(i)   Vary the power of a person to dissociate under Florida Statutes 605.0601, except to require that the notice under Statute 605.0602(1) be in a record.

(j)   Vary the grounds for dissolution specified in Florida Statutes 605.0702.

(k)   Vary the requirement to wind up the company's business, activities, and affairs as specified in Florida Statutes 605.0709(1), (2)(a), and (5).

(l)   Unreasonably restrict the right of a member to maintain an action under Florida Statutes 605.0801-605.0806.

(m)   Vary the provisions of Florida Statutes 605.0804 regarding special litigation committees.

(n)   Vary the right of a member to approve a merger, interest exchange, or conversion under Florida Statutes 605.1023(1)(b), 605.1033(1)(b), or 605.1043(1)(b), respectively.

(o)   Vary the required contents of plan of merger under Florida Statutes 605.1022, a plan of interest exchange under Statute 605.1032, a plan of conversion under Florida Statutes 605.1042, or a plan of domestication under Florida Statutes 605.1052.

(p)   Except as otherwise provided in Florida Statutes 605.0106 and 605.0107(2), restrict the rights under Chapter 605 of a person other than a member or manager.

(q)   Provide for indemnification for a member or manager under Florida Statutes 605.0408 for any of the following:

1.   Conduct involving bad faith, willful or intentional misconduct, or a knowing violation of law.

2.   A transaction from which the member or manager derived an improper personal benefit.

3.   A circumstance under which the liability provisions of Florida Statutes 605.0406 for improper distributions are applicable.

4.   A breach of duties or obligations under Florida Statutes 605.04091, regarding standards of conduct.

NOW, THEREFORE, in consideration of the mutual covenants and promises hereinafter set forth, the parties agree as follows:

ARTICLE I

DEFINITIONS

1.1 AFFILIATE. "Affiliate" means, when used with reference to a specified Person, (i) the Principal of the Person, (ii) any Person directly or indirectly controlling, controlled by or under common control with such Person, (iii) any Person owning or controlling 10% or more of the outstanding voting interests of such Person, and (iv) any relative or spouse of such Person.

1.2 AGREEMENT. "Agreement" means this Limited Liability Company Operating Agreement, as originally executed and as amended from time to time, as the context requires. Words such as "herein", "hereinafter", "hereto", "hereby" and "hereunder", when used with reference to this Agreement, refer to this Agreement as a whole, unless the context otherwise requires.

1.3 ARTICLES OF ORGANIZATION. "Articles of Organization" means the articles of organization filed with the Florida Secretary of State for the purpose of forming the Company.

1.4 AVAILABLE CASH FLOW. "Available Cash Flow" means, with respect to any Fiscal Year or other period, the sum of all cash receipts of the Company from any and all sources, less all cash disbursements (including loan repayments) and a reasonable allowance for Reserves, contingencies and anticipated obligations as determined by the Managers.

1.5 BUSINESS OF THE COMPANY. "Business of the Company" shall have the meaning set forth in Clause 2.7 hereof.

1.6 CAPITAL ACCOUNT. "Capital Account" of a Member shall have the meaning set forth in Article 3 hereof.

1.7 CAPITAL CONTRIBUTION. "Capital Contribution" shall have the meaning set forth in Article 3 hereof.

1.8 CODE. "Code" means the Internal Revenue Code, as amended (or any corresponding provision or provisions of any succeeding law).

1.9 DISSOLUTION. "Dissolution" means (i) when used with reference to the Company, the earlier of (a) the date upon which the Company is terminated under the Statute, or any similar provision enacted in lieu thereof, or (b) the date upon which the Company ceases to be a going concern, and (ii) when used with reference to any Member, the earlier of (a) the date upon which there is a Dissolution of the Company or (b) the date upon which such Member's entire interest in the Company is terminated by means of a distribution or series of distributions by the Company to such Member.

1.10 DISTRIBUTION. "Distribution" means the payment of some or all of the profits of the company to the members after the allocation of all profits and losses, and only upon determination by the members.

1.11 ECONOMIC INTEREST. "Economic Interest" means a Person's right to share in the Net Profits, Net Loss or similar items of, and to receive distributions from, the Company, but does not include any other rights of a Member including, without limitation, the right to vote or to participate in the management of the Company, or, except as provided in Clause 9.4, any right to information concerning the business and affairs of the Company.

1.12 FISCAL YEAR. "Fiscal Year" means the period of January 1 to and including December 31.

1.13 COMPANY. "Company" means [COMPANY NAME], LLC.

1.14 COMPANY INTEREST. "Company Interest" or "Interest" means an ownership interest in the Company, which includes the Economic Interest, the right to vote or participate in the management of Company, and the right to information concerning the business and affairs of the Company, as provided in this Agreement and under the Statute.

1.15 COMPANY LOANS. "Company Loans" shall

refer to any loans or advances made by any Member to the Company at the Member's option, without obligation to so do, to the extent the Company does not have sufficient resources (assets, borrowings or otherwise) to meet its Company obligations. Such Company Loans shall bear interest at the rate agreed to between the Member and the Managers.

1.16 MAJORITY IN INTEREST OF THE MEMBER. "Majority in Interest of the Member", unless otherwise provided in the Agreement, means more than fifty percent (50%) of the interests of the Member in the current profits of the Company.

1.17 MANAGERS. "Managers" means the Person elected to manage the Company pursuant to Clause 6.1 of this Agreement. At any time that the Members shall have elected to have more than one Manager, all such Persons so elected shall be referred to as the "Managers."

1.18 MEMBER. "Member" means a Person who:

1.18.1 Has been admitted to the Company as a member in accordance with the Articles of Organization or this Agreement, or an assignee of an Interest, other than an Economic Interest, who has become a Member pursuant to Clause 8.6.

1.18.2 Has not resigned, withdrawn or been expelled as a Member or, if other than an individual, been dissolved. Reference to a "Member" shall be to any one of the Member. Reference to an "Initial Member" shall be to any one of the Member listed in Clause 3.1.

1.19 NET CAPITAL CONTRIBUTIONS. "Net Capital

Contributions" means the aggregate of a Member's Capital Contributions over the aggregate distributions theretofore made to such Member pursuant to Clause 5.1.

1.20 NET PROFITS AND NET LOSS. "Net Profits" and "Net Loss" mean, for each Fiscal Year or other period, an amount equal to the Company's taxable income or loss for such year or period, determined in accordance with Code Section 703(a).

1.21 PERCENTAGE INTEREST. The Initial Members' "Percentage Interests" for voting matters shall be in the following percentages:

[Manager Name]   [percent interest]%

1.22 PERIOD OF DURATION. "Period of Duration" shall have the meaning set forth in Clause 2.6 hereof.

1.23 PERSON. "Person" means an individual, partnership, limited partnership, corporation, trust, estate, association, limited liability company, or other entity, whether domestic or foreign.

1.24 PRINCIPAL. 'Principal" means the natural Person which is in ultimate control of a Member.

1.25 PROPERTY. "Property" means all assets of the Company, both tangible and intangible, or any portion thereof.

1.26 RESERVES. "Reserves" means funds set aside from Capital Contributions or gross cash revenues as reserves. Such Reserves shall be maintained in amounts reasonably deemed sufficient by the Managers for working capital and the payment of taxes, insurance, debt service, repairs, replacements renewals, or other costs or expenses incident to the Business of the Company, or in the alternative, the Dissolution of the Company.

1.27 SECRETARY OF STATE. "Secretary of State" shall mean the Secretary of State of the State of Florida.

1.28 STATUTE. "Statute" shall mean Chapter 605 of the Florida Statutes.

1.29 TRANSFERABLE INTEREST. "Transferable interest" means the right, as initially owned by a person in the person's capacity as a member, to receive distributions from a limited liability company in accordance with the operating agreement, whether the person remains a member or continues to own a part of the right. The term applies to any fraction of the interest, by whoever owned.   Transferable Interest does not include voting rights, management rights or any other rights related to membership

1.30 VOTE. Except where superseded by another Clause of this Agreement, or required by the terms of the Statute or Code, all decisions made by the Company shall be approved by fifty-one percent (51%) of the votes ("Vote") of the Members, wherein each Member casts a number of votes equal to the Member's Percentage Interest in the Company.

   ARTICLE II
INTRODUCTORY MATTERS
2.1 FORMATION OF COMPANY. The parties have formed the Company pursuant to the provisions of the Statute by filing the Articles of Organization with the

Secretary of State.

2.2 NAME. The name of the Company is "[COMPANY NAME], LLC." The Members shall operate the Business of the Company under such name or use such other or additional names as the Member may deem necessary or desirable provided that: (i) no such name shall contain the words "bank", "insurance", "trust", "trustee", "incorporated", "Inc.", "corporation", "Corp.", or any similar name or variation thereof; (ii) the Members shall have reasonably determined, before use of any such name, that the Company is entitled to use such name and will not by reason of such use infringe upon any rights of any other Person, or violate any applicable laws or governmental regulations; and (iii) the Members shall register such name under assumed or fictitious name statutes or similar laws of the states in which the Company operates.

2.3 PRINCIPAL OFFICE. The principal place of business of the Company shall be [Company address], or at such other place as the Company may from time to time determine. The Company may maintain such other offices at such other places as the Company may deem advisable.

2.4 MAILING ADDRESS. The mailing address of business of the Company shall be [Mailing address], or at such other place as the Company may from time to time determine.

2.5 REGISTERED AGENT AND ADDRESS FOR SERVICE OF PROCESS. Pursuant to Florida law, the

Company shall maintain a registered agent and a registered office in Florida for the purpose of receiving service of process. The name and address of the Company's initial agent for service of process is:

_____, _____

_____. The registered agent may resign at any time upon giving written notice to the Company at its address as listed on the most recent Florida annual report. The Company may change its registered agent at any time. The Company shall notify the previous registered agent when a new registered agent is selected.

2.6 PERIOD OF DURATION. The period of duration of the Company ("Period of Duration") shall commence on the date of the filing of the Articles of Organization with the Florida Secretary of State, and shall continue indefinitely, unless the Company is terminated or dissolved sooner, in accordance with the provisions of this Agreement.

2.7 BUSINESS AND PURPOSE OF THE COMPANY. The business of the Company shall be [business purpose] and may conduct any other activity necessary or incidental to the foregoing in furtherance of the objects of the business of the Company. The Members may agree to expand the scope of the Company's business to include other projects and business activities, provided, however, the Company shall not conduct any banking, insurance or trust company business.

2.8 TRADEMARKS.

2.8.1 The parties acknowledge that the store logo and any trademarks not used by any individual member prior to the formation of the Company shall be deemed owned by the company. The Company shall register any such trademarks in its name with the Florida Department of State and/or the United States Patent and Trademark Office.

ARTICLE III

MEMBERS AND CAPITAL CONTRIBUTIONS

3.1 NAMES AND ADDRESSES OF INITIAL MEMBER. The names and addresses of the Initial Member are as follows:

3.1.1 [Member Name], whose address is [Member Address]

3.2 CONTRIBUTIONS. The Initial Member shall initially contribute the following to the Company:

3.2.1 [Member Name] shall provide: $[Initial contribution].   The total of the agreed value of [Member name] contribution shall be set at $[dividend percentage]

For the purpose of establishing the initial amount of each Member's capital account, the value of each Member's initial contribution shall be determined by mutual agreement.

A contribution may consist of tangible or intangible property or other benefit to a limited liability company, including money, services performed, promissory notes, other agreements to contribute money or property, and contracts for services to be performed only if agreed by the Members.   Any promise to make a contribution shall be placed in writing and signed by the contributing member.

Failure to make a required Capital Contribution shall result in a termination of all rights in the company.

3.3 ADDITIONAL CONTRIBUTIONS. Upon determination of the majority of members, additional contributions may be required based upon the needs of the company. Failure to make any required contribution shall result in a reduction of percentage interest in accordance with the amount of the Capital Contribution actually paid by the member in relation to the total Capital Contribution paid by all members either in cash or property.

3.4 RIGHTS WITH RESPECT TO CAPITAL.

3.4.1 Company Capital. No Member shall have the right to withdraw, or receive any return of, its Capital Contribution, and no Capital Contribution may be returned in the form of property other than cash except as specifically provided herein.

3.4.2 No Interest on Capital Contributions. Except as expressly provided in this Agreement, no Capital Contribution of any Member shall bear any interest or otherwise entitle the contributing Member to any compensation for use of the contributed capital.

3.4.3 Establishment of Capital Accounts. A separate capital account ("Capital Account") shall be maintained on the company books for each Member. For book purposes, each Member's Capital Account will be separated into a contribution account and an income (loss) account and will be maintained according to generally accepted accounting principles. Clauses 3.5 and 3.6 below describe the appropriate accounting treatment for tax purposes of the Capital Accounts.

3.5 GENERAL RULES FOR ADJUSTMENT OF CAPITAL ACCOUNTS. The Capital Account of each Member shall be:

3.5.1 Increases. Increased by:

(i) Such Member's cash contributions;

(ii) The agreed fair market value of property contributed by such Member (net of liabilities secured by such contributed property that the Company is considered to assume or take subject to under Code Section 752);

(iii) All items of Company income and gain (including income and gain exempt from tax) allocated to such Member pursuant to Article 4 or other provisions of this Agreement; and

3.5.2 Decreases. Decreased by:

(i) The amount of cash distributed to such Member;

(ii) The agreed fair market value of all actual and deemed distributions of property made to such Member pursuant to this Agreement (net of liabilities secured by such distributed property that the Member is considered to assume or take subject to under Code Section 752);

(iii) All items of Company deduction and loss allocated to such Member pursuant to Article 4 or other provisions of this Agreement.

3.6 SPECIAL RULES WITH RESPECT TO

CAPITAL ACCOUNTS. For purposes of computing the balance in a Member's Capital Account, no credit shall be given for any Capital Contribution which such Member is to make until such contribution is actually made. "Capital Contribution" refers to the total amount of cash and the agreed fair market value (net of liabilities) contributed to the Company by that Member and any subsequent contributions of cash and the agreed fair market value (net of liabilities) of any other property subsequently contributed to the Company by that Member.

3.7 TRANSFEREE'S CAPITAL ACCOUNT. In the event a Member, or the holder of an Economic Interest, transfers an Interest in accordance with the terms of this Agreement, the transferee shall succeed to the Capital Account of the transferor to the extent it relates to the transferred Interest.

3.8 COMPETING BUSINESS.   Except as otherwise expressly provided in this Agreement or the Act, neither the Members nor their shareholders, managers, officers, employees, partners, agents, family members or affiliates, shall be prohibited or restricted from investing in or conducting, either directly or indirectly, businesses of any nature whatsoever, including the ownership and operation of businesses similar to or in the same geographical area as those held by the Company; and any investment in or conduct of any such businesses by any such person or entity shall not give rise to any claim for an accounting by any Member or the Company or any right to claim any interest therein or the profits therefrom. Notwithstanding the foregoing, no Member shall take for any competing business, any advantage, merchandise or benefit that would appropriately belong to or be sold by the Company without first offering said advantage, merchandise or benefit to the Company.

3.9 RESIGNATION.   A person has the power to dissociate as a member at any time, rightfully or wrongfully, by withdrawing as a member by express will under Statute 605.0602(1). A person who wrongfully dissociates as a member is liable to the limited liability company and, subject to Statute 605.0801, to the other members for damages caused by the dissociation. The liability is in addition to each debt, obligation, or other liability of the member to the company or the other members.

A person is dissociated as a member if any of the following occur:

(1)   The company has notice of the person's express will to withdraw as a member, but if the person specified a withdrawal date later than the date the company had notice, on that later date.

(2)   An event stated in the operating agreement as causing the person's dissociation occurs.

(3)   The person's entire interest is transferred in a foreclosure sale under Statute 605.0503(5).

(4)   The person is expelled as a member pursuant to the operating agreement.

(5)   The person is expelled as a member by the

unanimous consent of the other members if any of the following occur:

(a)   It is unlawful to carry on the company's activities and affairs with the person as a member.

(b)   There has been a transfer of the person's entire transferable interest in the company other than:

1.   A transfer for security purposes; or

2.   A charging order in effect under Statute 605.0503 which has not been foreclosed.

(c)   The person is a corporation and:

1.   The company notifies the person that it will be expelled as a member because the person has filed articles or a certificate of dissolution or the equivalent, the person has been administratively dissolved, its charter or equivalent has been revoked, or the person's right to conduct business has been suspended by the person's jurisdiction of its formation; and

2.   Within 90 days after the notification, the articles or certificate of dissolution or the equivalent has not been revoked or its charter or right to conduct business has not been reinstated.

(d)   The person is an unincorporated entity that has been dissolved and whose business is being wound up.

(6)   On application by the company or a member in a direct action under Statute 605.0801, the person is expelled as a member by judicial order because the person:

(a)   Has engaged or is engaging in wrongful conduct that has affected adversely and materially, or will affect adversely and materially, the company's activities and affairs;

(b)   Has committed willfully or persistently, or is committing willfully and persistently, a material breach of the operating agreement or a duty or obligation under Statute 605.04091; or

(c)   Has engaged or is engaging in conduct relating to the company's activities and affairs which makes it not reasonably practicable to carry on the activities and affairs with the person as a member.

(7)   In the case of an individual:

(a)   The individual dies; or

(b)   A guardian or general conservator for the individual is appointed; or

(c)   There is a judicial order that the individual has otherwise become incapable of performing the individual's duties as a member under Chapter 605 or the operating agreement.

(8)   The person:

(a)   Becomes a debtor in bankruptcy;

(b)   Executes an assignment for the benefit of creditors; or

(c)   Seeks, consents to, or acquiesces in the appointment of a trustee, receiver, or liquidator of the person or of all or substantially all the person's property.

(9)   In the case of a person that is a testamentary or inter vivos trust or is acting as a member by virtue of being a trustee of such a trust, the trust's entire transferable interest in the company is distributed.

(10)   In the case of a person that is an estate or is

acting as a member by virtue of being a legal representative of an estate, the estate's entire transferable interest in the company is distributed.

(11) In the case of a person that is not an individual, the existence of the person terminates.

(12) The company participates in a merger under Statutes 605.1021-605.1026 and:

(a) The company is not the surviving entity; or

(b) Otherwise as a result of the merger, the person ceases to be a member.

(13) The company participates in an interest exchange under Statutes 605.1031-605.1036, and the person ceases to be a member.

(14) The company participates in a conversion under Statutes 605.1041-605.1046, and the person ceases to be member.

(15) The company dissolves and completes winding up.

3.10 DEATH. Upon the death of a member during the existence of the Limited Liability Company, the surviving or remaining members shall have the right to continue the Limited Liability Company business by themselves or with any other person or persons they may select. The deceased Members share net profits shall be paid to their estate/heirs for a period of one year, after which, the surviving Members shall purchase from the estate all of the right, share, and interest of the deceased member and assume all of the then existing liabilities of the Limited Liability Company.

3.11 EXPULSION. Any member may be expelled from the Limited Liability Company for fraudulent behavior on behalf of the Limited Liability Company, conviction of any crime, embezzlement, theft, or wrongful use of Limited Liability Company assets. The member may only be expelled upon the unanimous vote of all remaining members after thirty days' written notice to the member so affected. Any capital contributions remaining in the Limited Liability Company account after the expulsion of the member shall be repaid to the expelled member less damages incurred by the Limited Liability Company as a result of the actions of the expelled member.

3.12 DISABILITY. In the event that any member becomes physically or mentally incapable of continuing in the Limited Liability Company business, and such incapacity continues for a period of three (3) months, the other members may liquidate the Limited Liability Company or dissolve the Limited Liability Company and purchase the interest of the disabled member at book value.

For the first three (3) months of any disability, the disabled member shall be paid his regular salary; and for the following months the disabled member shall be paid one half of his regular salary.

ARTICLE IV

ALLOCATION OF PROFITS AND LOSSES

4.1 ALLOCATION OF NET PROFITS AND LOSSES. Except as otherwise provided in this Article 4, Net Profits and Net Loss of the Company in each

Fiscal Year shall be allocated among the Member as follows:

4.1.1 Net Profits. Net Profits shall be allocated among the Members as follows:

(i) first, to each of the Members until the cumulative Net Profits allocated to each Member pursuant to this Clause 4.1.1 is equal to the cumulative Net Loss allocated to the Member pursuant to Clause 4.1.2 for any prior period; and

(ii) thereafter, to the Member in accordance with their Percentage of the total Contribution as set out in Section 3.2 of this Operating Agreements.

4.1.2 Allocation of Net Loss. Except as otherwise provided in this Article 4, Net Loss shall be allocated among the Members as follows:

(i) first, to offset any Net Profits allocated pursuant to Clause 4.1.1.(i) hereof, and then to offset any Net Profits allocated pursuant to Clause 4.1.1(ii) hereof (in each case pro rata in proportion to their shares of Net Profits being offset);

(ii) second, in proportion to the positive balances, if any, in the Members' respective Capital Accounts, until such balances are reduced to zero; and

(iii) third, to the Members, pro rata, in accordance with their Percentage of the total Contribution as set out in Section 3.2 of this Operating Agreements.

4.2 RESIDUAL ALLOCATIONS. Except as otherwise provided in this Agreement, all items of Company income, gain, loss, deduction, and any other allocation not otherwise provided for shall be divided among the

Member in the same portion as they share Net Profits or Net Losses, as the case may be, for the Fiscal Year.

4.3 FEES TO MEMBER OR AFFILIATES. Notwithstanding the provisions of Clause 4.1, in the event that any fees, interest, or other amounts paid to any Member or any Affiliate thereof pursuant to this Agreement or any other agreement between the Company and any Member or Affiliate thereof providing for the payment of such amount, and deducted by the Company in reliance on Section 707(a) and/or 707(c) of the Code, are disallowed as deductions to the Company on its federal income tax return and are treated as Company distributions, then:

4.3.1 the Net Profits or Net Loss, as the case may be, for the Fiscal Year in which such fees, interest, or other amounts were paid shall be increased or decreased, as the case may be, by the amount of such fees, interest, or other amounts that are treated as Company distributions; and

4.3.2 there shall be allocated to the Members to which (or to whose Affiliate) such fees, interest, or other amounts were paid, prior to the allocations pursuant to Clause 4.1, an amount of gross income for the Fiscal Year equal to the amount of such fees, interest, or other amounts that are treated as Company distributions.

4.4 SECTION 704(c) ALLOCATION. Any item of income, gain, loss, and deduction with respect to any property (other than cash) that has been contributed by a Member to the capital of the Company and which is required or permitted to be allocated to such Member for income tax purposes under Section 704(c) of the Code so as to take into account the variation between the tax basis of such property and its fair market value at the time of its contribution shall be allocated to such Member solely for income tax purposes in the manner so required or permitted.

4.5 PROFIT PARTICIPATIONS.   Any transfer of a Transferable Interest shall give the transferee a right to receive profit participation, if and when the Members or Managers determine to pay distributions. No member shall have the right to demand a profit distribution without a vote of the majority in interest of the member.

ARTICLE V

DISTRIBUTIONS

5.1 AVAILABLE CASH FLOW. Unless otherwise agreed by the Members, available Cash Flow of the Company shall be distributed to the Members in accordance with the following priority and agreements:

5.1.1 First. Pro rata among the Members, in the ratio of the principal loan balances outstanding, until all of the accrued but unpaid interest on all Company Loans, if any, has been paid, and then the principal amounts thereof.

5.1.2 Second. To the Members, pari passu, on a pro rata basis, until all Net Capital Contributions are reduced to zero.

5.1.3 Third. To the Members in accordance with their applicable Percentage of the total Contribution as set out in Section 3.2 of this Operating Agreement as of the time of such distribution.

5.2 TIMING OF DISTRIBUTIONS. Distributions, including the payment of principal and interest of any company loan made of a member, may be made at any time by vote of the members, however no distribution may be made if

(a) The company would not be able to pay its debts as they become due in the ordinary course of the company's activities and affairs; or

(b) The company's total assets would be less than the sum of its total liabilities, plus the amount that would be needed if the company were to be dissolved and wound up at the time of the distribution, to satisfy the preferential rights upon dissolution and winding up of members and transferees whose preferential rights are superior to those of persons receiving the distribution. Determination of insolvency will be determined based upon the rules set out in Florida Statute 605.0405.

5.3 RIGHT TO DISTRIBUTION A member has a right to a distribution before the dissolution and winding up of a limited liability company only if the company decides to make an interim distribution. A member's dissociation does not entitle the person to a distribution. A member does not have a right to demand or receive a distribution from a limited liability company in a form other than money.

5.4 LIABILITY FOR IMPROPER DISTRIBUTION. Any member or manager who consents to a distribution made in violation of this agreement or Florida Statute 605.0405 may be held personally liable to the company for the amount of the distribution which exceeds the amount that could have been lawfully distributed. Personal liability is waived as to those members or manager who did not vote for such distribution.

ARTICLE VI

RIGHTS, DUTIES, OBLIGATIONS AND COMPENSATION OF MANAGERS AND OFFICERS

6.1 MANAGERS. Upon the formation of the Company, the Members have determined that the Company shall be [Manager Managed][Member Managed]. The initial manager shall be [Manager Name] and [second manager] (referred to hereinafter as the "Manager" or "Managers"). The Managers shall have such rights, duties and powers as are specified in this Agreement, or conferred upon the Managers by Vote of the Member. Pursuant to Florida Statute 605.0109, on behalf of the Company, the Manager has the power to do all things necessary or convenient to carry out the activities and affairs of the Company, including the power to do all of the following:

(1) Sue, be sued, and defend in its name.

(2) Purchase, receive, lease, or otherwise acquire, own, hold, improve, use, and otherwise deal with real or personal property or any legal or equitable interest in property, wherever located.

(3) Sell, convey, mortgage, grant a security interest in, lease, exchange, and otherwise encumber or dispose of all or a part of its property.

(4)   Purchase, receive, subscribe for, or otherwise acquire, own, hold, vote, use, sell, mortgage, lend, grant a security interest in, or otherwise dispose of and deal in and with, shares or other interests in or obligations of another entity.

(5)   Make contracts or guarantees or incur liabilities; borrow money; issue notes, bonds, or other obligations, which may be convertible into or include the option to purchase other securities of the limited liability company; or make contracts of guaranty and suretyship which are necessary or convenient to the conduct, promotion, or attainment of the purposes, activities, and affairs of the limited liability company.

(6)   Lend money, invest or reinvest its funds, and receive and hold real or personal property as security for repayment.

(7)   Conduct its business, locate offices, and exercise the powers granted by Chapter 605 within or without this state.

(8)   Select managers and appoint officers, directors, employees, and agents of the limited liability company, define their duties, fix their compensation, and lend them money and credit.

(9)   Make donations for the public welfare or for charitable, scientific, or educational purposes.

(10)   Pay pensions and establish pension plans, pension trusts, profit-sharing plans, bonus plans, option plans, and benefit or incentive plans for any or all of its current or former managers, members, officers, agents, and employees.

(11)   Be a promoter, incorporator, shareholder, partner, member, associate, or manager of a corporation, partnership, joint venture, trust, or other entity.

(12)   Make payments or donations or conduct any other act not inconsistent with applicable law which furthers the business of the limited liability company.

(13)   Enter into interest rate, basis, currency, hedge or other swap agreements, or cap, floor, put, call, option, exchange or collar agreements, derivative agreements, or similar agreements.

(14)   Grant, hold, or exercise a power of attorney, including an irrevocable power of attorney

6.1.1 Duties of the Managers. The Managers have, subject to the control of the Members, general supervision, direction, and control of the business of the Company. The Managers shall have the general powers and duties of management typically vested in the office of president of a corporation, and such other powers and duties as may be prescribed by the Members.

6.1.2 Election. The Managers of the Company shall be chosen annually by the Vote of the Members. In voting for the Managers, each Member shall have a number of votes equal to its Percentage of the total Contribution as set out in Section 3.2 of this Operating Agreement in the Company. The candidate for the Managers position who obtains the majority of Member votes cast shall succeed to that Managers position. The Managers shall hold office until the Managers resign or shall be removed.

6.1.3 Delegation.    The Manager shall not have the power and authority to delegate to one or more other persons the Manager's rights and powers to manage and control the business and affairs of the limited liability company, including the power and authority to delegate to agents, boards of managers, members, or directors, officers and assistant officers, and employees of a member or manager of the limited liability company, and the power and authority to delegate by a management agreement or similar agreement with, or otherwise to other persons, unless agree to by a majority vote of the members. The delegation by the Manager will not cause the Manager to cease to be the Manager of the Company.

6.2 CO-MANAGERS. If there should be chosen Co-Managers of the Company, the following provisions of this Clause 6.2 shall govern the manner in which the Co-Managers shall manage the Business of the Company, subject to provisions contained in other parts of this Agreement with respect to the transactions specifically enumerated therein.

6.2.1 The Co-Managers shall share in the duties described in Clause 6.1.1.

6.2.2 Meetings of the Managers shall be held at the principal office of the Company, unless some other place is designated in the notice of the meeting. Any Managers may participate in a meeting through use of a conference telephone, electronic means such as Skype, or similar communication equipment so long as all Managers participating in such a meeting can hear one another. Accurate minutes of any meeting of the Managers shall be maintained by the officer designated by the Managers for that purpose.

6.2.3 Regular meetings of the Managers shall be held immediately following the adjournment of the annual meeting of the Members at which the Managers are elected. No notice need be given of such regular meetings.

6.2.4 Special meetings of the Managers for any purpose may be called at any time by any Managers. At least (forty-eight) (48) hours' notice of the time and place of a special meeting of the Managers shall be delivered personally to the Managers or personally communicated to them by an officer of the Company by telephone, telegraph or facsimile. If the notice is sent to a Manager by letter, it shall be addressed to the Managers at the Manager's last known business address as it is shown on the records of the Company. In case such notice is mailed, it shall be deposited in the United States mail, first-class postage, prepaid, in the place in which the principal office of the Company is located at least five (5) days prior to the time of the holding of the meeting. Such mailing, telegraphing, telephoning, faxing or delivery as above provided shall be considered due, legal and personal notice to such Managers.

6.2.5 With respect to a special meeting which has not been duly called or noticed pursuant to the provisions of Clause 6.2.4, all transactions carried out at the meeting are as valid as if had at a meeting regularly called and noticed if: (i) all Managers are present at the meeting, and sign a written consent to the holding of such meeting; or (ii) if a majority of the Managers are present and if those not present sign a waiver of notice of such meeting or a consent to the holding of the meeting or an approval of the minutes thereof, whether prior to or after the holding of such meeting, which waiver, consent or approval shall be filed with the other records of the Company; or (iii) if a Managers attends a meeting without notice and does not protest prior to the meeting or at its commencement that notice was not given to him or her.

6.2.6 Any action required or permitted to be taken by the Managers may be taken without a meeting and will have the same force and effect as if taken by a vote of Managers at a meeting properly called and noticed, if authorized by a writing signed individually or collectively by all, but not less than all, the Managers. Such consent shall be filed with the records of the Company.

6.2.7 All of the total number of incumbent Managers shall be necessary to constitute a quorum for the transaction of business at any meeting of the Managers, and except as otherwise provided in this Agreement or by the Statute, the action of a majority of the Managers present at any meeting at which there is a quorum, when duly assembled, is valid. A meeting at which a quorum is initially present may continue to transact business, notwithstanding the withdrawal of Managers, if any action taken is approved by a majority of the required quorum for such meeting.

6.3 LIMITATIONS ON RIGHTS AND POWERS. Except by the unanimous agreement of the Members which is evidenced in a writing, and except as otherwise specifically provided in this Agreement, neither the Managers nor any other officer of the Company shall have authority to:

6.3.1 Enter into or commit to any agreement, contract, commitment or obligation on behalf of the Company obligating any Member or Principal to find additional capital, to make or guarantee a loan or to increase its personal liability either to the Company or to third parties;

6.3.2 Receive or permit any Member or Principal to receive any fee or rebate, or to participate in any reciprocal business arrangements that would have the effect of circumventing any of the provisions hereof;

6.3.3 Materially alter the Business of the Company or deviate from any approved business plan of the Company as set forth in this Agreement;

6.3.4 Permit or cause the Company to place title to any Property in the name of a nominee;

6.3.5 Permit the Company's funds to be commingled with the funds of any other Person;

6.3.6 Do any act in contravention of this Agreement;

6.3.7 Do any act which would make it impossible to carry on the Business of the Company;

6.3.8 Confess a judgment against the Company;

6.3.9 Possess Property, or assign rights in specific

Property, for other than a Company purpose;
6.3.10 Admit any person as a Member, except as otherwise provided in this Agreement;
6.3.11 Sell, lease, pledge, hypothecate, or grant a security interest in any Property, except in the ordinary course of business;
6.3.12 Attempt to dissolve or withdraw from the Company; and
6.3.13 Invest or reinvest any proceeds from the operation of the Company, or the sale, refinancing or other disposition of any Property.
6.4 COMPENSATION OF MANAGERS. The Company shall pay to the Managers such salary and other benefits as shall be approved from time to time by Vote of the Members. The Company shall reimburse the Managers for any expenses of the Managers that are properly to be borne by the Company.
6.5 COMPENSATION OF MEMBERS. Except as expressly permitted by this Agreement or any other written agreement, the Company shall pay no compensation to any Member or any Principal of any Member for their services to the Company.
6.6 EXPENSE REIMBURSEMENT. The Company shall reimburse the Members for any expenses paid by them that are properly to be borne by the Company, as approved from time to time by the Managers.
6.7 STATEMENT OF AUTHORITY. The limited liability company may file a statement of authority with the Department of State and the County Clerk's

Office setting forth the name of the company as it appears on the records of the department, the street and mailing addresses of its principal office; the authority or limitations on the authority of any persons based on their status or holding such position to execute an instrument transferring real property held in the name of the company; or enter into other transactions on behalf of, or otherwise act for or bind, the company; and may state the authority or limitations on the authority of a specific person to execute an instrument transferring real property held in the name of the company; or enter into other transactions on behalf of, or otherwise act for or bind, the company. The Company may also amend or cancel a statement of authority filed with the department. The Statement of Authority shall be valid for a specified period, no longer than five (5) years.

ARTICLE VII

MEMBERS' MEETINGS

7.1 PLACE OF MEETINGS. Meetings of the Members shall be held at the principal office of the Company, unless some other appropriate and convenient location, either within or without the state where the Articles of Organization were filed, shall be designated for that purpose from time to time by the Managers. All Members must appear in person or by electronic means.

7.2 ANNUAL MEETINGS OF MEMBERS. Unless changed by consent of the members, an annual meeting of the Members shall be held, each year, on the anniversary of the date of this Agreement, at 10:00 a.m. If this day shall be a legal holiday, then the meeting shall be held on the next succeeding business day, at the same time. At the annual meeting, the Members shall elect the Managers (or Managers), consider the valuation of membership units, determine compensation of officers and managers, discuss the strategic plan, determine the tax matters member, develop exit strategies and dissolution issues, and transact such other business as may be properly brought before the meeting.

7.3 SPECIAL MEETINGS. Special meetings of the Members may be called at any time by the Managers or by one or more Members holding in the aggregate more than ten percent (10%) of the Percentage Interests. Upon receipt of a written request, which request may be mailed or delivered personally to the Managers, by any Person entitled to call a special meeting of Members, the Managers shall cause notice to be given to the Members that a meeting will be held at a time requested by the Person or Persons calling the meeting, which time for the meeting shall be not less than ten (10) nor more than sixty (60) days after the receipt of such request. If such notice is not given within twenty (20) days after receipt of such request, the Persons calling the meeting may give notice thereof in the manner provided by this Agreement.

7.4 NOTICE OF MEETINGS. Except as provided for in Clause 7.3 for special meetings, notice of meetings shall be given to the Members in writing not less than ten (10) nor more than sixty (60) days before the date of the meeting by the Managers. Notices for regular and special meetings shall be given personally, by mail, or by facsimile, and shall be sent to each Member's last known business address appearing on the books of the Company. Such notice shall be deemed given at the time it is delivered personally, or deposited in the mail, or sent by facsimile. Notice of any meeting of Members shall specify the place, the day and the hour of the meeting, and (i) in case of a special meeting, the general nature of the business to be transacted, or (ii) in the case of an annual meeting, those matters which the Managers, at the date of mailing, intends to present for action by the Members.

7.5 VALIDATION OF MEMBERS' MEETINGS. The transactions of a meeting of Members which was not called or noticed pursuant to the provisions of Clause 7.3 or 7.4 shall be valid as though transacted at a meeting duly held after regular call and notice, if all Members are present, and if, either before or after the meeting, each of the Members entitled to vote at the meeting signs a written waiver of notice, or a consent to the holding of such meeting, or an approval of the minutes thereof. All such waivers, consents or approvals shall be filed with the records of the Company. Attendance shall constitute a waiver of notice, unless objection shall be made.

7.6 ACTIONS WITHOUT A MEETING.

7.6.1 Any action which may be taken at any annual or special meeting of Members may be taken without a meeting and without prior notice if a consent in writing, setting forth the action so taken, shall be signed by Members holding in the aggregate the number of votes equal to or greater than the Vote, unless a lesser vote is provided for by this Agreement or the Statute; provided, however, that any action which by the terms of this Agreement or by the Statute is required to be taken pursuant to a greater vote of the Members may only be taken by a written consent which has been signed by Members holding the requisite number of votes.

7.6.2 Unless the consents of all Members have been given in writing, notice of any approval made by the Members without a meeting by less than unanimous written consent shall be given at least ten (10) days before the consummation of the action authorized by such approval. Any Member giving a written consent may revoke the consent by a writing received by the Company prior to the time that written consents of Members required to authorize the proposed action have been filed with the Company. Such revocation is effective upon its receipt by the Company.

7.7 QUORUM AND EFFECT OF VOTE. Each Member shall have a number of votes equal to the Percentage Interest held by such Member, provided that if, pursuant to the Statute or the terms of this Agreement, a Member is not entitled to vote on a specific matter, then such Member's number of votes and Percentage Interest shall not be considered for purposes of determining whether a quorum is present, or whether approval by Vote of the Members has been obtained, in respect of such specific matter. Attendance of all Members shall constitute a quorum at all meetings of the Members for the transaction of business, and the Vote of Members shall be required to approve any action, unless a greater vote is required or a lesser vote is provided for by this Agreement or by the Statute.

ARTICLE VIII
RESTRICTIONS ON TRANSFER OR CONVERSION OF COMPANY INTERESTS, ADDITIONAL CAPITAL CONTRIBUTIONS; ADMISSION OF NEW MEMBER

8.1 TRANSFER OR ASSIGNMENT OF MEMBER'S INTEREST. The Transferable Interest of each Member and the Economic Interest of a Person who is not a Member constitutes personal property of the Member or Economic Interest holder. Each Member and each Economic Interest holder has no interest in the Property.

8.1.1 A Member's Transferable Interest or an Economic Interest may be transferred or assigned only as provided in this Agreement.

8.1.2 A Transfer of a Transferable Interest may be done without the consent of the other Members or of the Managers. Any holder of a Transferable Interest shall have no right to participate in the management of the business and affairs of the Company or to become a Member thereof.

8.1.3 Prior to making a transfer, the Transferring

Member shall first offer to transfer the Transferable Interest to the LLC on the same terms and conditions as offered to any third party. In the event the LLC does not choose to exercise the right of first refusal within 15 days, the Transferring Member shall next offer to transfer the Transferable Interest to the other members on the same terms and conditions as offered to any third party. If no member chooses to exercise the second right of refusal, the Member may then offer to transfer the Transferable Interest to a third party on terms no more favorable than that offered to the LLC or other members.

8.2 VOID TRANSFERS. Any Transfer of a Transferable Interest which does not satisfy the requirement of Clause 8.1.2 shall be void.

8.3 ADDITIONAL CAPITAL. During the Period of Duration, each of the Members shall be required to make additional Capital Contributions to the Company if such additional Capital Contributions are approved by Members holding, in the aggregate, seventy-five percent (75%) or more of the Percentage of the total Contribution as set out in Section 3.2 of this Operating Agreements.

8.3.1 Each Member shall be obligated to contribute an amount of additional capital equal to such Member's Percentage of the total Contribution as set out in Section 3.2 of this Operating Agreement times the total Capital Contribution amount required of all Members.

8.3.2 The Members' Percentage of the total Contribution as set out in Section 3.2 of this Operating

Agreements shall be adjusted to recognize any Member's failure to make the required additional Capital Contribution.

8.3.3 Any Member who fails to contribute some or all of the required additional capital shall be in default of this Agreement and shall have no right to participate in the management of the business and affairs of the Company, but such Member shall not forfeit its right to distributions and Net Profit and Net Loss allocations.

8.4     MAJOR DECISIONS; DEADLOCK; BUY-SELL AGREEMENT.

(a)     For purposes of this Section, the term "Major Decision" shall mean any action (or election not to act) by or on behalf of the Company which, pursuant to the provisions of this Agreement, requires the approval of all or a majority of the Members or the Management Committee, and which may have, or which may be anticipated to have, a material effect on the business and operation of the Company.

(b)     In the event the voting rights of the Members or the Management Committee are evenly divided with respect to a Major Decision and the Members or the Management Committee are unable to reach agreement with respect to a proposed course of action within fifteen (15) days after a request for action by any Member, then in such an event, a deadlock (the "Deadlock") shall be deemed to exist.

(c)     At any time after the occurrence of a Deadlock and prior to a resolution thereof among the

Members or the Management Committee, as applicable, or at any time after the commencement of operations (whether or not a Deadlock exists), either Member (the "Offering Member") may, upon written notice to the other Member (the "Offering Notice"), propose a Total Value which would be the basis for calculating the applicable Offering Price at which the Offering Member is willing to either (i) sell to the other Member all of the Offering Member's Interest or (ii) purchase from the other Member all of the other Member's Interest; provided however, that such Total Value shall not be less than an amount sufficient to repay the outstanding balance of principal and accrued but unpaid interest at 5% per annum of the other Member's Capital Contribution as set out in Section 3.2 of this Operating Agreement. The other Member shall have a period of thirty (30) days after delivery of the Offering Notice in which to elect, by written notice to the Offering Member (the "Response Notice") to either (i) purchase all of the Interest of the Offering Member at the applicable Offering Price or (ii) sell all of its Interest to the Offering Member at the applicable Offering Price. The failure of the other Member to duly and timely give a Response Notice shall constitute its election to sell all of its Interest to the Offering Member at the applicable Offering Price. Unless otherwise approved by the Members, such purchase and sale shall be consummated within nine (9) months after the expiration of the 15-day notice period and at least thirty percent (30%) of the purchase price for the

Interest being sold or purchased shall be payable at the closing in cash (or by wire transfer in immediately available funds).   The balance of the purchase price shall be paid in five (5) equal annual installments of principal, together with interest on the unpaid principal balance, and shall be secured by an assignment of all rights to receive any proceeds from distributions paid by the LLC.   Notwithstanding any other provisions hereof to the contrary, any Member shall not be required to close on the purchase of any Interest in accordance with this Section unless the representations and warranties of the selling Member as set forth in Section 8.4 shall be true and correct in all material respects as of the date of such closing, and the selling Member shall deliver a certificate to such effect to the purchasing party dated as of the closing date.

(d)   At any time after the occurrence of an Event of Default under this Agreement, the non-defaulting Member, without limiting any other rights or remedies it may have under this Agreement, any other agreement or instrument relating to or arising out of this Agreement, at law or in equity, may, upon written notice to the Defaulter (the "Appraisal Notice"), elect to either sell its Interest to the Defaulter or purchase the Interest of the Defaulter; provided however, that for purposes of determining the purchase price hereunder, the "Total Value" shall be an amount equal to the fair market value of the Company, as determined by mutual agreement of the Members or by appraisal.   If the Members are unable to mutually agree upon the fair market value of the Company within thirty (30) days after delivery of the Appraisal Notice, the non-defaulting Member shall select a reputable, disinterested appraiser who shall furnish the Members with a written Appraisal within thirty (30) days of the selection, setting forth the determination of the fair market value of the LLC as of the date of the Appraisal Notice.   Such Appraisal shall assume that the LLC shall be the highest and best use of the Property, shall assume that the assets are subject to any agreements, including without limitation, leases, management and service agreements then in effect, except this Agreement, and shall include the value of any licenses and similar intangible assets, but shall exclude any other intangible assets such as good will. The cost of the Appraisal shall be at the expense of the Defaulter.

8.5 DISSOCIATION.   Any Member who desires to withdraw from the Company must file a statement of dissociation containing the following:

(a)   The name of the limited liability company.

(b)   The name and signature of the dissociating member.

(c)   The date the member withdrew or will withdraw.

(d)   A statement that the company has been notified of the dissociation in writing.

The Company shall be authorized to forward this Statement of Dissociation to the Department of State. Upon dissociation, the dissociated member waives any further distribution rights, whether then owing or to be paid in the future.

8.6 ADMISSION OF NEW MEMBERS. A new Member may be admitted into the Company only upon the consent of all of the Members.

8.6.1 The amount of Capital Contribution which must be made by a new Member shall be determined by the vote of all existing Members.

8.6.2 A new Member shall not be deemed admitted into the Company until the Capital Contribution required of such Person shall have been made and such Person has become a party to this Agreement.

ARTICLE IX

BOOKS, RECORDS, REPORTS AND BANK ACCOUNTS

9.1 MAINTENANCE OF BOOKS AND RECORDS. The Company shall cause books and records of the Company to be maintained in accordance with Generally Accepted Accounting Principles, and shall give reports to the Members in accordance with prudent business practices and the Statute. There shall be kept at the principal office of the Company, as well as at the office of record of the Company specified in Clause 2.3, if different, the following Company documents:

9.1.1 A current list of the full name and last known business or residence address of each Member and of each holder of an Economic Interest in the Company set forth in alphabetical order, together with the Capital Contributions and share in Net Profits and Net Loss of each Member and holder of an Economic Interest;

9.1.2 A current list of the full name and business or residence address of each Manager;

9.1.3 A copy of the Articles of Organization and any amendments thereto, together with any powers of attorney pursuant to which the Articles of Organization and any amendments thereto were executed;

9.1.4 Copies of the Company's federal, state and local income tax or information returns and reports, if any, for the seven most recent Fiscal Years;

9.1.5 A copy of this Agreement and any amendments thereto, together with any powers of attorney pursuant to which this Agreement and any amendments thereto were executed;

9.1.6 Copies of the financial statements of the Company, if any, for the seven most recent Fiscal Years;

9.1.7 The Company's books and records as they relate to the internal affairs of the Company for at least the current and past five Fiscal Years;

9.1.8 Originals or copies of all minutes, actions by written consent, consents to action and waivers of notice by Members and Member Votes, actions and consents; and

9.1.9 Any other information required to be maintained by the Company pursuant to the Statute.

9.2 ANNUAL ACCOUNTING. Within 120 days after the close of each Fiscal Year of the Company, the Company shall (i) cause to be prepared and submitted to each Member a balance sheet and income statement for the preceding Fiscal Year of the Company (or portion thereof) in conformity with Generally Accepted Accounting Principles and (ii) provide to the Members all information necessary for them to complete federal and state tax returns.

9.3 INSPECTION AND AUDIT RIGHTS. Each Member has the right upon reasonable request, to inspect and copy during normal business hours at the Member's cost any of the Company books and records. Such right may be exercised by the Person or by that Person's agent or attorney. Any Member may require a review and/or audit of the books, records and reports of the Company. The determination of the Managers as to adjustments to the financial reports, books, records and returns of the Company, in the absence of fraud or gross negligence, shall be final and binding upon the Company and all of the Members.

9.4 RIGHTS OF MEMBERS AND NON-MEMBERS. Upon the request of a Member or a holder of an Economic Interest who is not a Member, for purposes reasonably related to the interest of that Person, the Managers shall promptly deliver to the Members or holder of an Economic Interest, at the expense of the Company, a copy of this Agreement and a copy of the information listed in this Agreement.

9.5 BANK ACCOUNTS. The bank accounts of the Company shall be maintained in such banking institutions as the Managers shall determine. Any expense in excess of $500.00 will require a vote of the majority interest in the Company.

9.6 TAX MATTERS HANDLED BY MANAGERS.

One of the Managers who is also a Member, or in the event no Managers are a Member, a Member or an officer of a corporate Member, shall be designated as "Tax Matters Partner" (as defined in Code section 6231), to represent the Company (at the Company's expense) in connection with all examinations of the Company's affairs by tax authorities, including resulting judicial and administrative proceedings, and to expend Company funds for professional services and costs associated therewith. In its capacity as "Tax Matters Partner", the designated Person shall oversee the Company tax affairs in the overall best interests of the Company. Unless the Members designate another to be "Tax Matters Partner", the Managers shall be the "Tax Matters Partner", provided that Person is a Member or an officer of a corporate Member.

9.7 FEDERAL INCOME TAX ELECTIONS MADE BY MANAGERS. The Managers on behalf of the Company may make all elections for federal income tax purposes, including but not limited to, the following:

9.7.1 Use of Accelerated Depreciation Methods. To the extent permitted by applicable law and regulations, the Company may elect to use an accelerated depreciation method on any depreciable unit of the assets of the Company; and

9.7.2 Adjustment of Basis of Assets. In case of a transfer of all or part of the Interest of any Member, the Company may elect, pursuant to Code Sections 734, 743, and 754, to adjust the basis of the assets of the

Company.

9.7.3 Accounting Method. For financial reporting purposes, the books and records of the Company shall be kept on the cash method of accounting applied in a consistent manner in accordance with Generally Accepted Accounting Principles and shall reflect all transactions of the Company and be appropriate and adequate for the purposes of the Company.

9.8 OBLIGATIONS OF MEMBERS TO REPORT ALLOCATIONS. The Members are aware of the income tax consequences of the allocations made by this Agreement and hereby agree to be bound by the provisions of this Clause 9.8 in reporting their shares of the Company income and loss for income tax purposes.

ARTICLE X

TERMINATION AND DISSOLUTION

10.1 DISSOLUTION. The Company shall be dissolved upon the occurrence of any of the following events:

10.1.1 An event or circumstance that the operating agreement states causes dissolution.

10.1.2 By the written approval of a Majority In Interest of the Members to dissolve the Company;

10.1.3 The passage of 90 consecutive days during which the company has no members, unless:

(a)    Consent to admit at least one specified person as a member is given by transferees owning the rights to receive a majority of distributions as transferees at the time the consent is to be effective; and

(b)    At least one person becomes a member in

accordance with the consent.

10.1.4 The entry of a decree of judicial dissolution in accordance with Statute 605.0705.

10.1.5 The filing of a statement of administrative dissolution by the department pursuant to Statute 605.0714.

10.2 ARTICLES OF DISSOLUTION. As soon as possible after the occurrence of any of the events specified in Clause 10.1 above, the Company shall execute Articles of Dissolution in such form as prescribed by the Secretary of State.

10.3 CONDUCT OF BUSINESS. Upon the filing of the Articles of Dissolution with the Secretary of State, the Company shall cease to carry on its business, except insofar as may be necessary for the winding up of its business, but the Company's separate existence shall continue until the Statement of Termination has been filed with the Secretary of State or until a decree dissolving the Company has been entered by a court of competent jurisdiction.

10.4 DISTRIBUTION OF NET PROCEEDS. The Members shall continue to divide Net Profits and Losses and Available Cash Flow during the winding-up period in the same manner and the same priorities as provided for in Articles 4 and 5 hereof. The proceeds from the liquidation of Property shall be applied in the following order:

10.4.1 To the payment of creditors, in the order of priority as provided by law, except to Member on account of their contributions;

10.4.2 To the payment of loans or advances that may have been made by any of the Member or their Principals for working capital or other requirements of the Company;

10.4.3 To the Member in accordance with the positive balances in their Capital Accounts after adjustments for all allocations of Net Profits and Net Loss.

Where the distribution pursuant to this Clause 10.4 consists both of cash (or cash equivalents) and non-cash assets, the cash (or cash equivalents) shall first be distributed, in a descending order, to fully satisfy each category starting with the most preferred category above. In the case of non-cash assets, the distribution values are to be based on the fair market value thereof as determined in good faith by the liquidator, and the shortest maturity portion of such non-cash assets (e.g., notes or other indebtedness) shall, to the extent such non-cash assets are readily divisible, be distributed, in a descending order, to fully satisfy each category above, starting with the most preferred category.

ARTICLE XI

INDEMNIFICATION OF THE MEMBERS, MANAGERS, AND THEIR AFFILIATES

11.1 INDEMNIFICATION OF THE MEMBERS AND THEIR PRINCIPALS. The Company shall indemnify and hold harmless the Members, the Managers, their Affiliates and their respective officers, directors, employees, agents and Principals (individually, an "Indemnitee") from and against any and all losses, claims, demands, costs, damages, liabilities, joint and several, expenses of any nature (including reasonable attorneys' fees and disbursements), judgments, fines, settlements and other amounts arising from any and all claims, demands, actions, suits or proceedings, whether civil, criminal, administrative or investigative, in which the Indemnitee was involved or may be involved, or threatened to be involved, as a party or otherwise, arising out of or incidental to the Business of the Company, excluding liabilities to any Member, regardless of whether the Indemnitee continues to be a Member, an Affiliate, or an officer, director, employee, agent or Principal of the Member at the time any such liability or expense is paid or incurred, to the fullest extent permitted by the Statute and all other applicable laws. Notwithstanding the above, the Company shall not indemnify a Member or Manager for any of the following:

1. Conduct involving bad faith, willful or intentional misconduct, or a knowing violation of law.

2. A transaction from which the member or manager derived an improper personal benefit.

3. A circumstance under which the liability provisions of Florida Statute 605.0406 for improper distributions are applicable.

4. A breach of duties or obligations under Florida Statute 605.04091, regarding standards of conduct.

11.2 EXPENSES. Expenses incurred by an Indemnitee in defending any claim, demand, action, suit or proceeding subject to Clause 11.1 shall, from time to time, be advanced by the Company prior to the final disposition of such claim, demand, action, suit or proceeding only if the person promises to repay the company in the event that the person ultimately is determined not to be entitled to be indemnified.

11.3 INDEMNIFICATION RIGHTS NON-EXCLUSIVE. The indemnification provided by Clause 11.1 shall be in addition to any other rights to which those indemnified may be entitled under any agreement, vote of the Members, as a matter of law or equity or otherwise, both as to action in the Indemnitee's capacity as a Member, as an Affiliate or as an officer, director, employee, agent or Principal of a Member and as to any action in another capacity, and shall continue as to an Indemnitee who has ceased to serve in such capacity and shall inure to the benefit of the heirs, successors, assigns and administrators of the Indemnitee.

11.4 ERRORS AND OMISSIONS INSURANCE. The Company may purchase and maintain insurance, at the Company's expense, on behalf of the Members and such other Persons as the Members shall determine, against any liability that may be asserted against, or any expense that may be incurred by, such Person in connection with the activities of the Company and/or the Members' acts or omissions as the Members of the Company regardless of whether the Company would have the obligation to indemnify such Person against such liability under the provisions of this Agreement.

11.4.1 Other Insurance. The Members agree that the

Company shall maintain liability insurance coverage in the amount of at least One Million Dollars ($1,000,000). The Members further agree that the Company may obtain General Liability and D&O Insurance coverage in appropriate amounts.

11.5 ASSETS OF THE COMPANY. Any indemnification under Clause 11.1 shall be satisfied solely out of the assets of the Company. No Member shall be subject to personal liability or required to fund or to cause to be funded any obligation by reason of these indemnification provisions.

ARTICLE XII

ISSUANCE OF COMPANY CERTIFICATES

12.1 ISSUANCE OF COMPANY CERTIFICATES. The interest of each Member in the Company shall be represented by a Company Certificate. Upon the execution of this Agreement and the payment (or other provision) of the Capital Contributions by the Member pursuant to Clause 3.2 hereof, the Managers shall cause the Company to issue one or more Company Certificates in the name of each Member certifying that the Person named therein is the record holder of the Company Units set forth therein. For purposes of this Agreement, the term "record holder" shall mean the person whose name appears in Clause 1.21 as the Member owning the Company Interest at issue.

12.2 TRANSFER OF COMPANY CERTIFICATES. A Member's Transferable Interest which is transferred in accordance with the terms of Clause 8.1 of this Agreement shall be transferable on the books of the

Company by the record holder thereof in person or by such record holder's duly authorized attorney. The Managers shall issue to the transferee a [COMPANY NAME], LLC Certificate representing the Transferable Interest.

12.3 LOST, STOLEN OR DESTROYED CERTIFICATES. The Company shall issue an [COMPANY NAME], LLC Certificate in place of any Company Certificate previously issued if the record holder of the Company Certificate:

12.3.1 Makes proof by affidavit, in form and substance satisfactory to the Managers, that a previously issued Company Certificate has been lost, destroyed or stolen;

12.3.2 Requests the issuance of an [COMPANY NAME], LLC Certificate before the Company has notice that the Company Certificate has been acquired by a purchaser for value in good faith and without notice of an adverse claim;

12.3.3 If requested by the Managers, delivers to the Company a bond, in form and substance reasonably satisfactory to the Managers, with such surety or sureties and with fixed or open penalty as the Managers may direct, in the Managers' reasonable discretion, to indemnify the Company against any claim that may be made on account of the alleged loss, destruction or theft of the Company Certificate; and

12.3.4 Satisfies any other reasonable requirements imposed by the Managers.

If a Member fails to notify the Company within a reasonable time after it has notice of the loss, destruction or theft of a Company Certificate, and a transfer of the Company Interest represented by the Company Certificate is registered before receiving such notification, the Company shall have no liability with respect to any claim against the Company for such transfer or for an [COMPANY NAME], LLC Certificate.

ARTICLE XIII

AMENDMENTS

13.1 AMENDMENT, ETC. OF OPERATION AGREEMENT. This Agreement may be adopted, altered, amended, or repealed and a new operating agreement may be adopted by a Majority In Interest of the Membership. Any modification to this Operating Agreement MUST be in writing. In the event any litigation arises regarding this Operating Agreement or any part thereof, the Court shall look solely to the plain language of this Operating Agreement and shall not consider extraneous issues such as course of conduct in interpreting the terms of the Operating Agreement.

13.2 AMENDMENT, ETC. OF ARTICLES OF ORGANIZATION. Notwithstanding any provision to the contrary in the Articles of Organization or this Agreement, in no event shall the Articles of Organization be amended without the vote of Member representing a Majority In Interest of the Member.

ARTICLE XIV

MISCELLANEOUS PROVISIONS

14.1 COUNTERPARTS. This Agreement may be executed in several counterparts, and all counterparts so executed shall constitute one Agreement, binding on all of the parties hereto, notwithstanding that all of the parties are not signatories to the original or the same counterpart. All signatures to this Operating Agreement may be made electronically, by facsimile, conformed copy, digitally or by any other reproducible means.

14.2 SURVIVAL OF RIGHTS. This Agreement shall be binding upon, and, as to permitted or accepted successors, transferees and assigns, inure to the benefit of the Members and the Company and their respective heirs, legatees, legal representatives, successors, transferees and assigns, in all cases whether by the laws of descent and distribution, merger, reverse merger, consolidation, sale of assets, other sale, operation of law or otherwise.

14.3 SEVERABILITY. In the event any Clause, or any sentence within any Clause, is declared by a court of competent jurisdiction to be void or unenforceable, such sentence or Clause shall be deemed severed from the remainder of this Agreement and the balance of this Agreement shall remain in full force and effect.

14.4 NOTIFICATION OR NOTICES. Except for notices to be given under Articles 6 and 7 for purposes of meetings of Managers and meetings of Member, any notice or other communication required or permitted hereunder shall be in writing and shall be deemed to have been given if personally delivered, transmitted by facsimile (with mechanical confirmation of transmission), or deposited in the United States mail, registered or certified, postage prepaid, addressed to the parties' addresses set forth below. Notices given in the manner provided for in this Clause 14.4 shall be deemed effective on the third day following deposit in the mail or on the day of transmission or delivery if given by facsimile or by hand. Notices must be addressed to the parties hereto at the following addresses, unless the same shall have been changed by notice in accordance herewith.

14.5 CONSTRUCTION. The language in all parts of this Agreement shall be in all cases construed simply according to its fair meaning and not strictly for or against any of the Members.

14.6 CLAUSE TITLES. The captions of the Articles or Clauses in this Agreement are for convenience only and in no way define, limit, extend or describe the scope or intent of any of the provisions hereof, shall not be deemed part of this Agreement and shall not be used in construing or interpreting this Agreement.

14.7 GOVERNING LAW. This Agreement shall be construed according to the laws of the state of Florida. The law of the state of Florida governs the internal affairs of the limited liability company and the liability of a member as member, and a manager as manager, for the debts, obligations, or other liabilities of the limited liability company.

14.8 ADDITIONAL DOCUMENTS. Each Member, upon the request of another Member, agrees to perform all further acts and execute, acknowledge and deliver all documents which may be reasonably necessary, appropriate or desirable to carry out the provisions of this Agreement, including but not limited to acknowledging before a notary public any signature heretofore or hereafter made by a Member.

14.9 PRONOUNS AND PLURALS. Whenever the context may require, any pronoun used in this Agreement shall include the corresponding masculine, feminine and neuter forms, and the singular form of nouns, pronouns and verbs shall include the plural and vice versa.

14.10 TIME OF THE ESSENCE. Except as otherwise provided herein, time is of the essence in connection with each and every provision of this Agreement.

14.11 FURTHER ACTIONS. Each of the Members agrees to execute, acknowledge and deliver such additional documents, and take such further actions, as may reasonably be required from time to time to carry out each of the provisions, and the intent, of this Agreement, and every agreement or document relating hereto, or entered into in connection herewith.

14.12 ARBITRATION OF DISPUTES. Any Member hereto may require the arbitration of any dispute arising under or in connection with this agreement or any related agreement. Such Member may initiate and require arbitration by giving notice to the other parties specifying the matter to be arbitrated. If legal action is already pending on any matter concerning which the notice is given, the notice shall not be effective unless given by the defendant therein and given before the expiration of twenty (20) days after service of process on the person giving the notice. Except as provided to the contrary in these provisions on arbitration, the arbitration shall be in conformity with and subject to applicable rules and procedures of the American Arbitration Association (or any successor thereto). If the American Arbitration Association is not then in existence and there is no successor, or if for any reason the American Arbitration Association fails or refuses to act, the arbitration shall be in conformity with and subject to the provisions of applicable Florida statutes (if any) relating to arbitration at the time of the notice. The arbitrators shall be bound by this agreement and all related agreements. Pleadings in any action pending on the same matter shall, if arbitration is required as aforesaid, be deemed amended to limit the issues to those contemplated by the rules prescribed above. Each Member shall pay the costs of arbitration, including arbitrator's fees, as awarded by the arbitrator(s). The number and selection of arbitrator(s) shall be in accordance with the rules prescribed above, except that (i) each arbitrator selected shall be neutral and familiar with the principal subject matter of the issues to be arbitrated, such as, by way of example, entertainment industry projects, or such other subject matter as may be at issue, (ii) the testimony of witnesses shall be given under oath, and (iii) depositions and other discovery may be ordered by the arbitrator(s).

14.13 WAIVER OF JURY. With respect to any dispute arising under or in connection with this agreement or any related agreement, as to which no member invokes the right to arbitration hereinabove provided, or as to which legal action nevertheless occurs, each Member hereby irrevocably waives all rights it may have to demand a jury trial. This waiver is knowingly, intentionally, and voluntarily made by the Member and each Member acknowledges that none of the other Members or any person acting on behalf of the other parties has made any representation of fact to induce this waiver of trial by jury or in any way modified or nullified its effect. The Member each further acknowledge that it has been represented (or has had the opportunity to be represented) in the signing of this Agreement and in the making of this waiver by independent legal counsel, selected of its own free will, and that it has had the opportunity to discuss this waiver with counsel. The Members each further acknowledge that it has read and understands the meaning and ramifications of this waiver provision.

14.14 THIRD PARTY BENEFICIARIES. There are no third party beneficiaries of this Agreement except (i) Affiliates and Principals of the Member and (ii) any other Persons as may be entitled to the benefits of Clause 11.1 hereof.

14.15 TAX ELECTIONS. The Managers, in the Managers' sole discretion, shall cause the Company to make or not make all elections required or permitted to be made for income tax purposes.

14.16 PARTITION. Except as specifically provided herein, the Members agree that the Property that the Company may own or have an interest in is not suitable for partition. Each of the Members hereby irrevocably waives any and all rights that it may have to maintain any action for partition of any Property the Company may at any time have an interest in.

14.17 ENTIRE AGREEMENT. This Agreement (including any attachments) and the Articles of Organization constitute the entire agreement of the Members with respect to, and supersedes all prior written and oral agreements, understandings and negotiations with respect to, the subject matter hereof.

14.18 WAIVER. No failure by any party to insist upon the strict performance of any covenant, duty, agreement or condition of this Agreement or to exercise any right or remedy consequent upon a breach thereof shall constitute a waiver of any such breach or any other covenant, duty, agreement or condition.

14.19 ATTORNEYS' FEES. In the event of any litigation, arbitration or other dispute arising as a result of or by reason of this Agreement, the prevailing party in any such litigation, arbitration or other dispute shall be entitled to, in addition to any other damages assessed, its reasonable attorneys' fees, and all other costs and expenses incurred in connection with settling or resolving such dispute. The attorneys' fees which the prevailing party is entitled to recover shall include fees for prosecuting or defending any appeal and shall be awarded for any supplemental proceedings until the final judgment is satisfied in full. In addition to the foregoing award of attorneys' fees to the prevailing party, the prevailing party in any lawsuit or arbitration procedure on this Agreement shall be entitled to its reasonable attorneys' fees incurred in any post-judgment proceedings to collect or enforce the judgment. This attorneys' fees provision is separate and several and shall survive the merger of this Agreement into any judgment.

14.20 CONFIDENTIALITY AND PRESS RELEASES. The Members and their respective Affiliates and Principals hereby agree that it is in all of their best interests to keep this Agreement and the Business of the Company and all information concerning such business confidential. Such parties each agree that they will not take any action nor conduct themselves in any fashion, including giving press releases or granting interviews, that would disclose to third parties unrelated to the Company the Business of the Company or any aspect of the Company without the unanimous prior written approval of all Members. To the extent such prior approval is given, it may be conditioned upon approval of the text of any press release or the scope of any intended interview.

14.21 LIMITATION OF ACTIONS. No litigation, arbitration or other action shall be filed or taken by any Member or Manager regarding any dispute over this Operating Agreement after one year has passed from the time the grounds of the dispute first arose.

IN WITNESS WHEREOF, the parties hereto have hereunto executed this Agreement as of the date first written above.

[Manager Name]

[second manager]

# APPENDIX 6: NonCompetition/ NonSoliciatation / Non-Disclosure Agreement

## NON-COMPETITION/NON-DISCLOSURE/NON-SOLICITATION AGREEMENT

THIS AGREEMENT is made this _____ day of _____, _____, by and between _____, whose mailing address is _____ hereinafter collectively referred to as "the Purchaser," and, _____ individually and as Members of, _____LLC, whose mailing address is hereinafter collectively referred to as "Seller," under the following circumstances:

### RECITALS

A.    On _____, the Purchaser and Seller entered into an Asset Purchase Agreement, hereinafter referred to as "the Purchase Agreement".

B.    The Purchase Agreement provides that the Purchaser and Seller will enter into this Non-Competition/ Non-

Disclosure/ Non-Solicitation Agreement at the closing of the transactions contemplated by the Purchase Agreement as an inducement to the Seller and Purchaser to enter into the Purchase Agreement.

C.     The value of the Business Assets would be severely affected and materially impaired if the Seller and the Purchaser were to enter into full competition with each other.

D.     The execution of this Non-Competition/ Non-Disclosure/ Non-Solicitation Agreement is a material condition to Purchaser's agreement to acquire the Business Assets and to Seller's agreement to sell the Business Assets.

**NOW THEREFORE,** for and in consideration of mutual covenants contained herein and other good and valuable considerations, the receipt and sufficiency of which are hereby acknowledged, the parties agree as follows:

### *Section 1.*     *Definitions and Recitals.*

Except as otherwise indicated, capitalized terms used herein are defined as set forth in the Purchase Agreement. As used in this Non-Competition Agreement, the following terms have the following meanings:

1.1 "Business"     means     that     business     known     as _____.

1.2 "Business Assets" means the assets of that business known as _____, transferred pursuant to the Asset Purchase Agreement.

1.3 "Confidential Information" means (I) any information with respect to the Purchaser's customers, accounts, costs, plans, business policies, programs, formulae, products, know-how, trade secrets, suppliers, pricing policies or rates, marketing techniques, or any other information which may now or in the future be considered by the Purchaser to be confidential or proprietary, (ii) reports, memoranda, correspondence, and other writings belonging to the Purchaser, which may have been produced by or come into the possession of the Purchaser or Seller in the course of its ownership or operation of the Business, excluding any of the foregoing which is in the public domain.

1.4 "Territory" means the State of Florida.

## Section 2.    Non-Competition.

2.1    In order that the Purchaser may obtain the full benefit of the sale and the goodwill related thereto, the Seller does hereby covenant and agree that for a period five (5) years after the closing of the Purchase Agreement, Seller shall not, directly or indirectly (as agent, consultant or otherwise) engage in the ownership, management, employment by or operation in any ways of a business providing _____ services throughout the Territory.

2.2    It is the intent of the parties that the provision of this section 2 shall be enforced to the fullest extent permissible under the laws and public policies applied in each jurisdiction in which enforcement is sought. Accordingly, to the extent that the Non-Competition restrictions hereunder shall be adjudicated to be invalid or unenforceable in any such jurisdiction, the court making such determination shall have the power to limit, construe or reduce the duration, scope, activity and/or area of such provision, and/or delete specific words or phrases to the extent necessary to render such provision enforceable to the maximum reasonable extent permitted by applicable law, such limited form to apply only with respect to the operation of this section in the particular jurisdiction in which such adjudication is made.

2.3     The parties are aware of Purchaser's business plan and acknowledge that the Territory is proper and appropriate.

### Section 3.     Nondisclosure.

Seller and Purchaser recognize and acknowledge that they have, and may acquire additional, knowledge of Confidential Information, and that such information constitutes valuable, special, and unique property of Purchaser and/or of Seller. Seller will not, at any time, disclose any such Confidential Information of Purchaser to any person, except as required by law. Seller acknowledges that the Confidential Information of the Business is material to the value of the Business, and is unique, and agrees that disclosure thereof in violation of this Agreement may irreparably damage the value of the Business.

### Section 4.     Nonsolicitation

For a period of five (5) years from the closing of the Purchase Agreement, Seller, individually, in a partnership with others, or in a corporation either existing or to be formed, will not, solicit any of the customers of Purchaser or any employee that worked for Seller or works for Purchaser.

### Section 5.     Injunctive Relief.

Seller and Purchaser acknowledge that their adherence to the terms of the covenants set forth in Sections 2 and 3 are necessary to protect the value of the Business Assets to the Purchaser, that a continuing breach of such covenants will result in irreparable and continuing damage to the value of the Business Assets, and that money damages would not adequately compensate the Purchaser for any such breach and, therefore, that the Purchaser would not have an adequate remedy at law. In the event any action or proceeding shall be instituted by the Purchaser to enforce any provision of Sections 2 or 3, the Seller shall waive the claim or defenses in such action that (i) money damages are adequate to compensate the Purchaser for such breach, and (ii) there is an adequate remedy at law available to the Purchaser, and shall not urge in any such action or proceeding the claim or defense that such remedy at law exists. The Purchaser shall have, in addition to any and all remedies at law and/or in equity, the right, without posting of bond or other security, to an injunction, both temporary and permanent, specific performance and/or other equitable relief to prevent the violation of any obligation under Sections 2 or 3. The parties agree that the remedies of the Purchaser for breach of Sections 2 or 3 shall be cumulative, and seeking or obtaining injunctive or other equitable relief shall not preclude the making of a claim for damages or other relief. The parties to this Agreement also agree that the Purchaser shall be entitled to such damages as the Purchaser can show they have sustained by reason of such breach and shall not be limited in its damages by any provision of the Purchase Agreement. In any action brought to enforce the covenants set forth in Section 2 or 3, or to recover damages for breach thereof, the prevailing party shall be entitled to recover reasonable attorneys' fees and other expenses of litigation, in all trial and appellate levels, together with such other and further relief as may be proper.

### Section 6.    Independent Agreement.

The covenants of Purchaser and Seller hereunder shall be construed to be independent of covenants, representations, warranties, and obligations of Purchaser and Seller under the Purchase Agreement or under any agreement, document, or instrument delivered pursuant to the Purchase Agreement and, accordingly, any default by the Purchaser or Seller with respect to any such representation, warranty, covenant, or obligation shall not constitute an excuse for any failure of Purchaser or Seller to perform hereunder.

### *Section 7.* *Waiver.*

The failure of any party to insist in any one or more instances upon performance of any of the provisions of this Non-Competition/Non-Disclosure/Non-Solicitation Agreement or to take advantage of any of its rights hereunder shall not be construed as a waiver of any such provisions or the relinquishment of any such rights, and the same shall continue and remain in full force and effect. No single or partial exercise by any party of any right or remedy shall preclude other or future exercise thereof or the exercise of any other right or remedy. Waiver by any party of any breach of any provision of this Non-Competition/Non-Disclosure/Non-Solicitation Agreement shall not constitute or be construed as a continuing waiver or as waiver of any other breach of any other provision of this Non-Competition/Non-Disclosure/Non-Solicitation Agreement.

### *Section 8.* *Notice.*

All notices, requests, demands, and other communications hereunder shall be in writing and shall be made by certified mail or telefax followed by confirmation letter (with first class airmail postage), to the parties at the addresses indicated below:

If to the Seller:

and

If to the Buyer:

All notices, demands and other communications mentioned above shall be deemed to have been given or made on the earlier of the date when received and five (5) days after the date of their dispatch. Any party may change the address to which notices and other communications are to be directed to it by giving notice of such change to the other parties in the manner provided in this Section.

## Section 9.    Severability.

If any provision of this Non-Competition/Non-Disclosure/Non-Solicitation Agreement, as applied to any person or to any circumstance, shall be adjudged by a court to be invalid or unenforceable, the same shall in no way affect any other provision of this Non-Competition/Non-Disclosure/Non-Solicitation Agreement, the application of such provision in any other circumstances, or the validity or enforceability of this Non-Competition/Non-Disclosure/Non-Solicitation Agreement.

## Section 10.    Amendment.

No waiver of any rights, and no modifications or amendment of this Non-Competition/Non-Disclosure/Non-Solicitation Agreement shall be effective unless made in writing and duly signed by the party to be bound thereby.

## Section 11.    Governing Law.

This Non-Competition/Non-Disclosure/ Non-Solicitation Agreement shall be construed according to and the legal relations between the parties shall be governed in accordance with the laws of the

State of Florida, as applicable to agreements executed and fully performed in the State of Florida.

### Section 12. Successors of Purchaser and Seller.

The terms of this Non-Competition/Non-Disclosure/Non-Solicitation Agreement shall inure to the benefit of the Purchaser and Seller and their respective successors or assigns.

### Section 13. Captions.

The captions contained in this Non-Competition/Non-Disclosure/Non-Solicitation Agreement are for convenience or reference only and shall not affect the meaning or interpretation of this Non-Competition/Non-Disclosure/Non-Solicitation Agreement.

### Section 14. Entire Agreement.

This Agreement contains the entire understanding of the parties hereto with respect to the subject matter hereof and shall supersede all previous, oral and written understandings of the parties with respect to the subject matter hereof

### Section 15. Jurisdiction.

The parties hereto intend to and do hereby confer jurisdiction to enforce this Non-Competition/Non-Disclosure/Non-Solicitation Agreement upon the courts of the State of Florida.

The undersigned have signed this Agreement to indicate and agree that they shall be bound by the terms and provisions of this Agreement.

IN WITNESS WHEREOF, the parties have executed this Non-Competition/Non-Disclosure/Non-Solicitation Agreement as of the date first written above.

Signed, sealed and delivered
in the presence of:

_____

# APPENDIX 7:
# EIN APPLICATION

# APPENDIX 7: EIN APPLICATION

Form **SS-4**
(Rev. December 2017)
Department of the Treasury
Internal Revenue Service

**Application for Employer Identification Number**
(For use by employers, corporations, partnerships, trusts, estates, churches, government agencies, Indian tribal entities, certain individuals, and others.)
▶ Go to www.irs.gov/FormSS4 for instructions and the latest information.
▶ See separate instructions for each line. ▶ Keep a copy for your records.

OMB No. 1545-0003
EIN

Type or print clearly.

1 Legal name of entity (or individual) for whom the EIN is being requested

2 Trade name of business (if different from name on line 1)
3 Executor, administrator, trustee, "care of" name

4a Mailing address (room, apt., suite no. and street, or P.O. box)
5a Street address (if different) (Do not enter a P.O. box.)

4b City, state, and ZIP code (if foreign, see instructions)
5b City, state, and ZIP code (if foreign, see instructions)

6 County and state where principal business is located

7a Name of responsible party
7b SSN, ITIN, or EIN

8a Is this application for a limited liability company (LLC) (or a foreign equivalent)? ☐ Yes ☐ No
8b If 8a is "Yes," enter the number of LLC members ▶

8c If 8a is "Yes," was the LLC organized in the United States? ☐ Yes ☐ No

9a **Type of entity** (check only one box). **Caution.** If 8a is "Yes," see the instructions for the correct box to check.
☐ Sole proprietor (SSN)
☐ Partnership
☐ Corporation (enter form number to be filed) ▶
☐ Personal service corporation
☐ Church or church-controlled organization
☐ Other nonprofit organization (specify) ▶
☐ Other (specify) ▶
☐ Estate (SSN of decedent)
☐ Plan administrator (TIN)
☐ Trust (TIN of grantor)
☐ Military/National Guard ☐ State/local government
☐ Farmers' cooperative ☐ Federal government
☐ REMIC ☐ Indian tribal governments/enterprises
Group Exemption Number (GEN) if any ▶

9b If a corporation, name the state or foreign country (if applicable) where incorporated | State | Foreign country

10 **Reason for applying** (check only one box)
☐ Started new business (specify type) ▶
☐ Hired employees (Check the box and see line 13.)
☐ Compliance with IRS withholding regulations
☐ Other (specify) ▶
☐ Banking purpose (specify purpose) ▶
☐ Changed type of organization (specify new type) ▶
☐ Purchased going business
☐ Created a trust (specify type) ▶
☐ Created a pension plan (specify type) ▶

11 Date business started or acquired (month, day, year). See instructions.
12 Closing month of accounting year

13 Highest number of employees expected in the next 12 months (enter -0- if none). If no employees expected, skip line 14.
Agricultural | Household | Other

14 If you expect your employment tax liability to be $1,000 or less in a full calendar year **and** want to file Form 944 annually instead of Forms 941 quarterly, check here. (Your employment tax liability generally will be $1,000 or less if you expect to pay $4,000 or less in total wages.) If you do not check this box, you must file Form 941 for every quarter. ☐

15 First date wages or annuities were paid (month, day, year). **Note:** If applicant is a withholding agent, enter date income will first be paid to nonresident alien (month, day, year) ▶

16 Check **one** box that best describes the principal activity of your business.
☐ Health care & social assistance ☐ Wholesale-agent/broker
☐ Construction ☐ Rental & leasing ☐ Transportation & warehousing ☐ Accommodation & food service ☐ Wholesale-other ☐ Retail
☐ Real estate ☐ Manufacturing ☐ Finance & insurance ☐ Other (specify) ▶

17 Indicate principal line of merchandise sold, specific construction work done, products produced, or services provided.

18 Has the applicant entity shown on line 1 ever applied for and received an EIN? ☐ Yes ☐ No
If "Yes," write previous EIN here ▶

**Third Party Designee**
Complete this section **only** if you want to authorize the named individual to receive the entity's EIN and answer questions about the completion of this form.
Designee's name | Designee's telephone number (include area code)
Address and ZIP code | Designee's fax number (include area code)

Under penalties of perjury, I declare that I have examined this application, and to the best of my knowledge and belief, it is true, correct, and complete.
Name and title (type or print clearly) ▶
Applicant's telephone number (include area code)
Applicant's fax number (include area code)
Signature ▶ Date ▶

**For Privacy Act and Paperwork Reduction Act Notice, see separate instructions.** Cat. No. 16055N Form **SS-4** (Rev. 12-2017)

# APPENDIX 8:
# IRS TWENTY POINT TEST FOR INDEPENDENT CONTRACTORS

The 20 factors identified by the IRS are as follows:

1. Instructions:   If the person for whom the services are performed has the right to require compliance with instructions, this indicates employee status.
2. Training:   Worker training (e.g., by requiring attendance at training sessions) indicates that the person for whom services are performed wants the services performed in a particular manner (which indicates employee status).
3. Integration:   Integration of the worker's services into the business operations of the person for whom services are performed is an indication of employee status.
4. Services rendered personally:   If the services are required to be performed personally, this is an indication that the person for whom services are performed is interested in the methods used to

accomplish the work (which indicates employee status).

5. Hiring, supervision, and paying assistants:    If the person for whom services are performed hires, supervises or pays assistants, this generally indicates employee status.    However, if the worker hires and supervises others under a contract pursuant to which the worker agrees to provide material and labor and is only responsible for the result, this indicates independent contractor status.

6. Continuing relationship:    A continuing relationship between the worker and the person for whom the services are performed indicates employee status.

7. Set hours of work:    The establishment of set hours for the worker indicates employee status.

8. Full time required:    If the worker must devote substantially full time to the business of the person for whom services are performed, this indicates employee status.    An independent contractor is free to work when and for whom he or she chooses.

9. Doing work on employer's premises:    If the work is performed on the premises of the person for whom the services are performed, this indicates employee status, especially if the work could be done elsewhere.

10. Order or sequence test:    If a worker must perform services in the order or sequence set by the person for whom services are performed, that shows the worker is not free to follow his or her own pattern of work, and indicates employee status.

11. Oral or written reports:    A requirement that the

worker submit regular reports indicates employee
status.

12. Payment by the hour, week, or month:    Payment
by the hour, week, or month generally points to
employment status; payment by the job or a
commission indicates independent contractor status.

13. Payment of business and/or traveling expenses:    If
the person for whom the services are performed pays
expenses, this indicates employee status.    An
employer, to control expenses, generally retains the
right to direct the worker.

14. Furnishing tools and materials:    The provision of
significant tools and materials to the worker indicates
employee status.

15. Significant investment:    Investment in facilities
used by the worker indicates independent contractor
status.

16. Realization of profit or loss:    A worker who can
realize a profit or suffer a loss as a result of the
services (in addition to profit or loss ordinarily realized
by employees) is generally an independent contractor.

17. Working for more than one firm at a time:    If a
worker performs more than de minimis services for
multiple firms at the same time, that generally indicates
independent contractor status.

18. Making service available to the general public:    If
a worker makes his or her services available to the
public on a regular and consistent basis, that indicates
independent contractor status.

19. Right to discharge:    The right to discharge a

worker is a factor indicating that the worker is an employee.

20. Right to terminate:   If a worker has the right to terminate the relationship with the person for whom services are performed at any time he or she wishes without incurring liability, that indicates employee status.

# ABOUT THE AUTHOR

**ALBERT L. KELLEY** is an attorney, author, book publisher, film producer, traveler and adventurer located in Key West, Florida. His law practice concentrates primarily in the areas of business, corporations, contracts, copyright, trademark, and entertainment law, as well as landlord-tenant law.

He graduated cum laude from Florida State University College of Law in 1989. He served for years as an adjunct professor for St. Leo University in their Business Administration program, teaching courses in business, employment and administrative law. Al has written a weekly business law newspaper column for well over ten years and has published books on business law, small claims court and landlord-tenant law. He has also been a featured panelist at Florida State University's College of Law's Annual Entertainment Art and Sports Law Symposium. Albert L. Kelley serves as legal counsel for the world's largest offshore powerboat race promoter as well as museums, art galleries, television stations, performers and newspapers. On the business side, Albert is corporate counsel to over 150 corporations, and has filed countless trademark and copyright applications. Albert has negotiated contracts with numerous national companies including Apple Computers, Harley Davidson, and Ralston Purina. He also is co-owner of Gee Whiz Entertainment, LLC- a multimedia corporation handling film, television and publishing ventures. Al has given numerous seminars on trademarks, copyrights, film licensing and financing, and foreclosure defenses. He is a licensed skydiver, hang-glider pilot, and scuba diver.

www.ingramcontent.com/pod-product-compliance
Lightning Source LLC
Chambersburg PA
CBHW070502200326
41519CB00013B/2682